a mended garment is

a little piece of artwork that you wear around all day, on display like a living gallery wall, eliciting comments, starting conversations, an opening sentence to a good story.

Mending Life

A Handbook for Repairing Clothes and Hearts

Sonya and Nina Montenegro

SASQUATCH BOOKS
SEATTLE

To all the people courageous enough
to sew a patch onto their clothes
and embark on a mending life.

+ + + + +

And to our ma, the original book maker,
whose love for books inspired us
to make our own.

+ + + + +

And to our pa, the original mender,
whose ingenious fixes sparked our
appreciation for mending.

The quality that we call beauty...
must always grow from
the realities of life.

—Jun'ichirō Tanizaki, *In Praise of Shadows*

I am not what I am,
I am what I do with my hands.

—Louise Bourgeois

Contents

+ + + + + + +

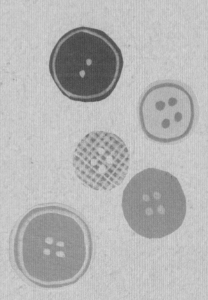

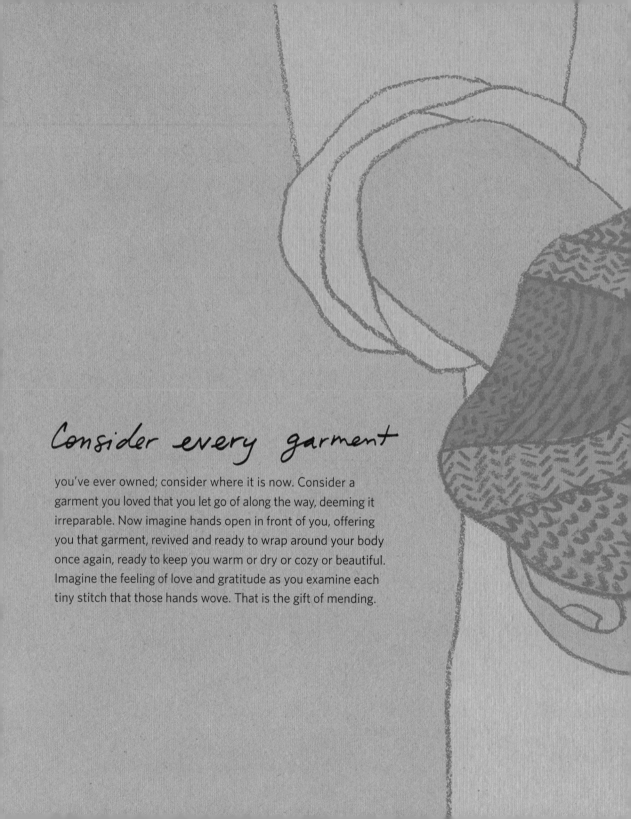

Consider every garment

you've ever owned; consider where it is now. Consider a garment you loved that you let go of along the way, deeming it irreparable. Now imagine hands open in front of you, offering you that garment, revived and ready to wrap around your body once again, ready to keep you warm or dry or cozy or beautiful. Imagine the feeling of love and gratitude as you examine each tiny stitch that those hands wove. That is the gift of mending.

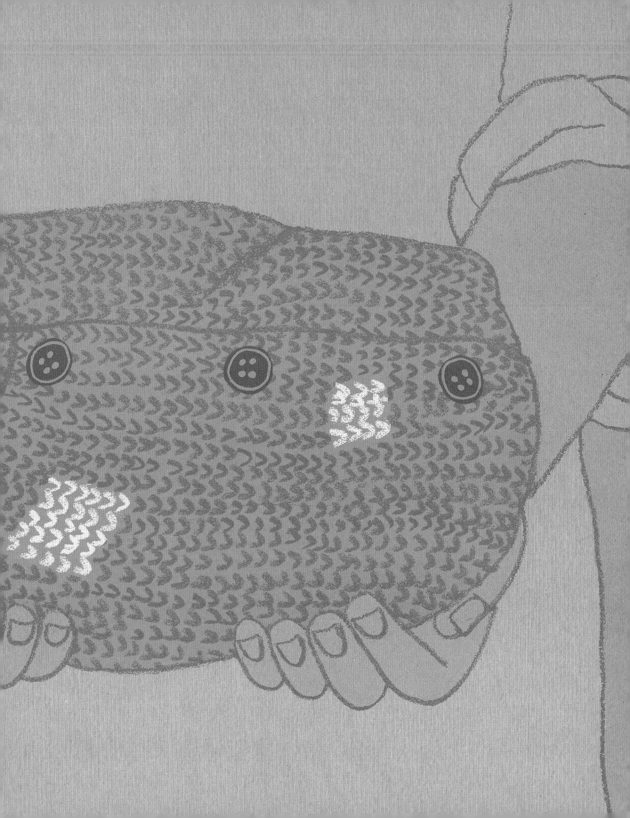

Introduction

We all wear clothes.

These clothes
tatter,
tear,
split,
run,
rip,
unravel,
spring holes.

Things fall apart.

But we are gifted
with hands that
sew,
mend,
fasten,
pin,
glue,
weave,
darn.

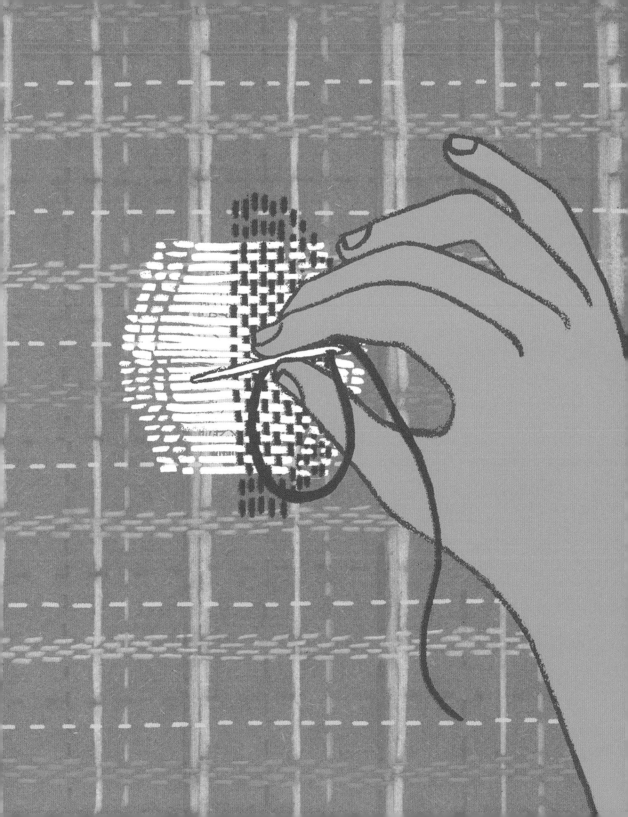

Things
come back
together.

Wounds heal.

Hearts forgive
and deepen with compassion.

Mending is a part of
being alive.

Why Mend?

+ + + + + + +

This book is an invitation to you, dear reader, to join the rekindling of an age-old practice. Mending was once a necessity—most people had only a few cherished garments—and to buy something new was expensive. Today it costs so little to purchase clothing that when a garment springs a hole it can be casually discarded and replaced. Yet much of the true cost of clothing made abroad is hidden, including environmental destruction and the dangerous conditions garment workers are subjected to. As our eyes open to these harsh realities, our hearts break. We wonder what we can do in the face of such enormous ecological and humanitarian crises.

At first glance, mending may seem inconsequential, but not only does it mean buying fewer new clothes (thus slowing down the fast fashion cycle), it also invites us into a new way of being. Mending is a powerful act of restoration, both for our clothes and for our relationship to the world. We mend in gratitude, honoring all that went into making our clothes: the people who labored to bring them into being, and the plants and animals that contributed to their creation. In taking care of that which takes care of us, we are demonstrating a deep understanding of our interconnectedness with every part of this world. When we sit down to mend, we cultivate a mindset that extends beyond clothing. Much like meditation, mending teaches us to embrace imperfection, and to practice patience and acceptance with ourselves. Through mending, we become accustomed to seeing our hand in the things we own. We become an active participant in their evolution.

Making something whole again is also a form of healing, and we humans have a deep desire to heal what is broken. Learning to mend

gives us a new lens through which to problem solve. A garment or belonging we thought was beyond repair is now stitched back together by our own two hands and we discover we are more resilient than we thought. We may even begin to see other opportunities for healing: we can make amends with someone we're at odds with, we can restore fertility to degraded soil, we can create a thriving urban oasis for pollinators, and with each small act, our broken hearts begin to heal in turn.

— — — — — — — — —

This handbook is meant to be passed around and passed down, just as the tradition of mending has been, across time and cultures. The threads that make up its warp and weft are personal reflections based on our own mending journey, and simple instructions for how to mend by hand. We, the authors, are self-taught menders, and because of this, we are confident that mending is a skill anyone can learn regardless of their level of sewing experience.

We have found that in mending, there is infinite room for experimentation, creativity, and play. There are many good ways! And while each mender will find their own unique style and rhythm, all menders are joined together in a beautiful act of restoration, an act with the power to mend both clothes and hearts.

"There are hundreds of ways
to kneel and kiss the ground."

— Rumi

Getting Started

Growing up, Sundays were special for Sonya and me. In the late after-noon we would head over to our grandparents' house for supper. As a casserole bubbled in the oven and our grandpa settled in to watch *Wheel of Fortune* while working on a crossword puzzle, our grandma Marion would sit on the couch with her basket full of mending supplies—darning mush-rooms, assorted needles, bits of yarn, colorful thread, and scraps of fabric already cut into neat squares with pinking shears. We'd have gathered our battered clothes for Grandma in advance—a pair of corduroys with a blown-out knee from falling off my bike, Sonya's cream-colored tights with a run in them from snagging on the tire swing. She would lovingly take them into her lap. "These holes make me happy," she would say. We'd give her a quizzical look—how could she be happy about ragged holes when they just gave her more work? "These holes tell a story. They tell me how much you two love to play; they tell me how full and rich your life is. Now let's fix these clothes with love, so that they can embrace you once again," Grandma would say.

The wheel spun and Vanna White flipped the tiles on the wall. "But how can you pay attention to the TV if you're always working, Grandma?" we would ask.

"I have one eye on the TV and one eye on my stitches," she would say with a wink. She never could just sit there and watch; her hands always had to be moving, busy, accomplishing something.

The years went by, and I never bothered to ask my grandmother to teach me her magic because it felt like she would always be there to take care of my things . . . but then she wasn't.

My first attempt at mending involved an enormous rip across the knee on a pair of beloved jeans that I had owned for eight years. The air was turning crisp, and this hole was inviting in such a gust of cold air with my every step that I was forced to do something about it. I nearly scissored off the legs to make shorts for summer, but something stopped me—a faint curiosity, a wondering: can I actually fix these?

I endeavored to find out. It was hard to keep my stitches tidy and the fabric flat; my fingers fumbled the straight pins, and when I finished and held the pants out to examine my work, the patch looked like the knobby, disfigured knot in a tree where a branch had broken off and the bark grew over. At first I lamented how messy and imperfect my work was, deeming the pants to be best made into shorts after all. But when I put them on, the patch was doing its job and it was doing it well. I wore those jeans with the asymmetrical patch and the uneven stitches with pride at having restored them with my own hands.

One short month later, my stitches tugged on the threadbare fabric surrounding the patch and opened a new hole, right above my previous mend. Frustrated, I sank down into the couch on a Sunday afternoon with my jeans on my lap to repair the new hole.

I chose a warm brown fabric and a brightly colored thread. Thoughts kept popping into my head: *Is this worth it? What if another hole springs up in just another month? This could be never-ending. . . . What time is it? How long am I going to have to work on this? What else could I be doing right now? Why don't I just buy a new pair of jeans?*

But I ignored those pesky thoughts. I thought of Sundays with our grandmother. I could see her sitting, patiently mending, never frustrated, always calm and forgiving of the holes and the clothes and the time it took to mend. As I handled the denim again, stitching on the second patch, the pants became more beautiful. This second patch looked better than the first. I was practicing. I was improving.

A while later, another hole *did* appear, but this time I didn't hesitate to get out my mending tools and choose a new patch to add. I breathed deeply and thought of how similar the work was to collage—intuitively adding layers of color and shape to make a composition I'd be wearing on my knee. In time, mending became a ritual for me, something I tucked into my backpack and took along everywhere to work on whenever I had a free moment. Just like our grandma, I came to understand that there is always time to mend.

—Nina

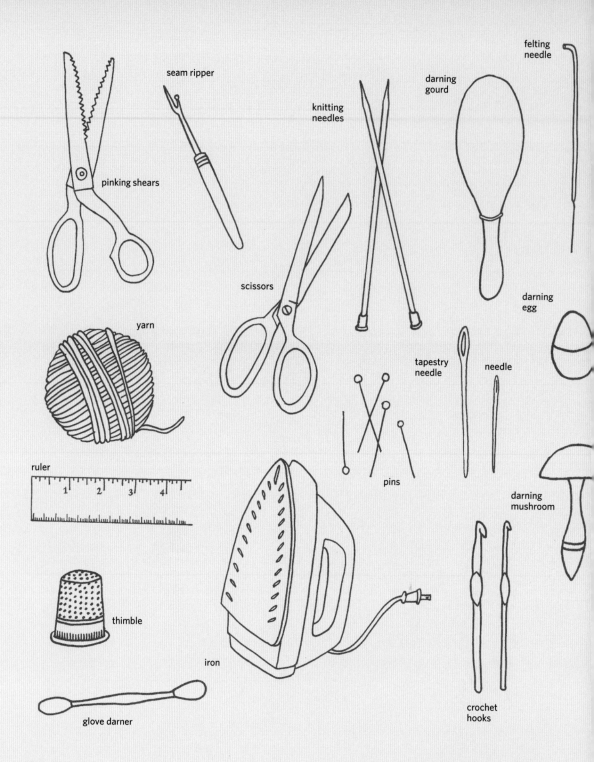

pinking shears

seam ripper

knitting needles

darning gourd

felting needle

scissors

yarn

tapestry needle

needle

darning egg

ruler

1   2   3   4

pins

darning mushroom

thimble

iron

crochet hooks

glove darner

6

wool
roving

fabric
pencil

Essential Supplies

+ + + + + + +

Sewing is a delight because, at its most basic, it requires very little to be able to do a lot: the only true essentials are a needle and thread. And, of course, having scissors is helpful too. You probably already have these three things at home somewhere (check the junk drawer). If you don't, ask around before you run out to buy all new supplies! Family and friends may have supplies languishing in attics, basements, or closets that they'd be happy to pass on to you. Keep an eye out at thrift stores, church rummage sales, garage sales, estate sales, antique shops, tool swaps, and community message boards. It can be helpful to gather a variety of supplies over time—such as different-colored yarn, fabric, and thread—to have lots to choose from when mending, whether it's to play and experiment or to match a mend to a garment. Here we outline the supplies that are handy to have at the ready to tackle the most common mending projects. In addition to this master list, each individual tutorial details which supplies and specialty tools are needed.

thread

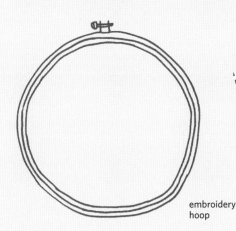

embroidery
hoop

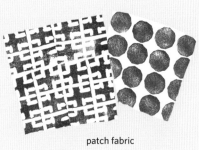

patch fabric

Fabric Pencil   For dark fabrics, white chalk pencil marks are most visible, while colored chalk pencils are best used on white fabrics. Chalk fabric pencils are water soluble and marks can generally be removed with a towel and water, or with water and mild soap. (For any marking tool, make sure to thoroughly read the instructions on the packaging and test beforehand on a scrap of fabric or small unseen area to make sure the mark washes out.)

Iron   Lightly used irons show up so often at thrift stores that we never see a reason to shop new. If you also choose to shop secondhand, just be sure the iron works and that its metal plate is clean (sometimes people use irons for craft projects, which can leave unwanted residue, such as wax or ink, on the iron face).

Needles   General-purpose hand-sewing needles (also known as sharps) are useful for most mending projects. They come in various thicknesses and lengths. It's helpful to have a couple of small (sizes 8 through 12, approximately 1 inch long) and medium (sizes 1 through 7, 1¼ to 2 inches long) needles. Experiment with different needle sizes; if it feels hard to pull your thread through the fabric, try a thicker needle with a larger eye. If you notice that your needle is making big holes in your fabric, try a thinner one with a smaller eye.

Other needles you might need depending on your mending project:

- **Sashiko needle**—Available in long or short: the long is recommended for sewing straight sashiko lines, whereas the short is for curved lines; alternatively, use a size 1 or 2 embroidery needle.

- **Tapestry needle**—Used for darning, it has a large eye to accommodate yarn and a blunt tip, so as to not split and weaken the yarn fibers.

Patch Fabric   It is helpful to have an assortment of fabrics to choose from when patching: denim, woven cotton, and knits. If you discover that a garment is past the point of repair, it can become patch material. The old garment will remain useful in your life. Smaller pieces of unique fabric—for example pillowcases or table linens, perfect for patches—can often be found in thrift stores, free piles, or the remnant bin at the fabric store.

Pinking Shears   These are scissors with sawtooth blades instead of straight. They make a zigzag cut, which minimizes fraying, and thus damage, to fabric. Only use pinking shears for cutting fabric because paper will quickly dull your scissors.

Pins   Straight pins are great for general use. Pins with glass or plastic heads are easier for beginners to manage. Silk pins are thinner and recommended for easily slipping into any fabric and not leaving visible holes.

Ruler   Any ruler will do, but we find a clear-plastic quilting ruler is easiest to use when drawing a grid onto fabric for decorative sashiko stitching. Find a ruler that's at least 12 inches long.

Scissors   Any sharp pair will do, but if you are able to buy a new pair of scissors and use them for *only* cutting fabric, do so! There is so much joy in cutting fabric with very sharp scissors. Cutting paper, cardboard, or wire with your scissors will dull them quickly. (Optional: it can be helpful to have a pair of small embroidery scissors for easily snipping threads and mending on the go.)

Seam Ripper   A seam ripper is a convenient cutting tool for quickly taking apart seams and errant stitches and for cutting threads.

Thimble This isn't an absolute necessity, but it's useful to protect the finger that is pushing the needle through the material when mending thick fabrics such as canvas or denim. You can find thimbles made from metal, plastic, silicon, or leather—choose whichever feels most comfortable.

Thread It's helpful to have a variety of thread in your collection. Common options include:

- **All-purpose**—A great general-use thread, made from polyester, cotton-wrapped polyester, or 100 percent cotton and available in a rainbow of colors. We prefer to use 100 percent cotton thread, which is all-natural (and will therefore biodegrade). For added strength and glide, the thread can be pulled across a block of beeswax before sewing. Polyester and cotton-wrapped polyester thread are synthetic petroleum-based products but are generally recommended for sewing knits and ensuring stronger seams.

- **Button and craft**—More durable and heftier than all-purpose. As its name implies, it is great for attaching buttons or for any project needing really strong thread, like mending a seam or repairing work wear. (A doubled all-purpose thread is a fine alternative to button and craft.)

- **Sashiko**—Matte white cotton is traditional (although other colors are available). Alternatively, you can use embroidery thread, which has more of a sheen, but is composed of many strands that can be separated for a thinner thread as desired.

Yarn Consider gathering a collection of yarns of varying weights, materials, and colors. If you're a knitter, hang on to any leftover yarn; shorter lengths are great for darning projects. Another way to source yarn for darning is to unravel a knitted garment (a hat, sweater, or scarf).

Specialty Supplies

+ + + + + + +

These supplies are less common than the Essential Supplies (page 7), but they also often pop up at yard sales, thrift stores, and antique malls. They are frequently overlooked because their use is not common knowledge any longer—but this also means they are often inexpensive. Finding high-quality vintage versions is a delight! A treasured tool in our collection is an old wooden darning egg that opens at the bulb to reveal a hidden compartment for storing needles and whatnot.

Crochet Hook If you will be making a crocheted patch (see page 76), we recommend having two hooks on hand: a small one, around 3 mm—especially if the garment has a tight knit—and a larger one, around 5 mm, to fill the hole more quickly.

Darning Egg This is a handy tool for mending an item with dimension, such as a sock—the egg holds the shape of a heel or toe while darning so it won't stretch or pucker. Alternatively, common household items work too: an orange, apple, lemon, gourd, or light bulb. Anything smooth, round, and hard will make a perfectly good darning tool.

Darning Mushroom and Gourd These are similar to an egg with the addition of a neck or "handle." This handle is useful for gathering extra material around to hold taut when darning, and can also double as a glove darner.

Embroidery Hoop A hoop is useful when darning a flat item (such as a sweater, blanket, shawl, or hat) because it holds the garment flat and taut. Find one approximately 6 to 8 inches in diameter (or smaller, if you can find one! A smaller hoop is helpful for mending more awkward areas, like a sweater elbow). Some menders find a hoop helpful for patching too!

- - - - - - -

Felting Needle   This is a barbed needle about 3 inches long that is made specifically for the needle-felting technique (see page 82). Available at many craft stores and online.

- - - - - - -

Glove Darner   This has a small bulbous end to insert into a glove finger for mending.

- - - - - - -

Knitting Needles   If you will be knitting a patch (see page 79), you will need a pair of knitting needles. The size will depend on the yarn you choose, but as a general rule, use smaller knitting needles for lightweight yarn and larger needles for chunkier, heavyweight yarn.

- - - - - - -

Wool Roving A long fluffy rope of unspun wool fiber, wool roving is used for making a needle-felted patch (see page 82). You can find it new at a craft store (or online) and it is available in many colors. Or, get resourceful and pull apart 100 percent wool yarn bits (leftover from projects or even from unraveling an old wool sweater) to make the fluffy roving yourself.

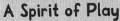

A Spirit of Play

We approach mending with a spirit of play and experimentation, inspired by our pa, a carpenter and artist by trade and an overall mastermind at fixing things. Our parents' home is full of inventive mends: wooden chairs mended by rejoining split rungs with a sturdy wrapping of thread secured with glue; a wide vintage sofa our pa rescued from an alley and experimentally reupholstered twenty years ago; a rip from the cat's claw in our screen door patched with a square of mesh and wire thread. When we were younger, it was a bit embarrassing when friends would come over and see a wooden handle affixed to the refrigerator where the sleek plastic original had been or a mismatched knob on the dresser drawer, but later on we came to appreciate and be proud of Pa's ingenuity.

A few of Pa's personal possessions show the same inventiveness: a missing screw on the arm of a pair of glasses is replaced with thin wire, and his watchband is sewn together where it tore in half. He always chooses red thread when he mends something. It's a bold move. His brown leather belt has bright red stitches where it broke, and the mend is obvious, whereas with brown thread it would have been much less visible. This is a conscious choice to make the garment look more interesting. There is an honesty in recognizing he could never renew it to a completely flawless state, so why not mend in a way that adds intrigue, *celebrating* the flaw instead of hiding it?

With his red thread, our pa unknowingly practices a version of *kintsugi*, the Japanese art of "golden joinery." Kintsugi is the ancient practice of fixing a broken piece of pottery with gold lacquer, highlighting the mend instead of trying to hide it. Inevitable accidents and mistakes thus become opportunities to remake an item into something more beautiful and unique.

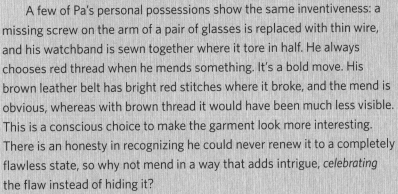
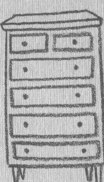

Pa says he doesn't necessarily set out to fix things to save money or for the sake of our environment, although both are important outcomes of a repair. Rather, it is the intellectual challenge of fixing the things he uses that inspires him. When something breaks, he sees it as a chance to play.

Mending on the Go

Mending is such sweet, portable work—it is quiet and does not interfere with conversation. One's mind wanders as stitches are sewn, listening to the sounds of the world, turning inward to thoughts, ideas, musings. Moving hands are a lot like moving feet: "Methinks that the moment my legs begin to move, my thoughts begin to flow," said Henry David Thoreau. Somehow in these movements, thoughts untangle, crimps of the mind iron out, new mental paths are forged. It's in these in-between moments, when the body is busy (weeding, bathing, biking, sewing), that the mind clears. These are the moments when ideas pay a visit.

Mending cultivates patience and calm. It can keep you content—it is the perfect thing to do while waiting—because it soothes antsy, fussy feelings with quiet productiveness. Is it so bad to be "on hold" for what feels like an eternity (on the phone, in the waiting room, at the airport) if you are able to darn a sock and finally pair it with its lonely mate?

Whether riding on the train to work, attending a book club meeting, or waiting at the DMV, you may be surprised to find that you do have time and space in the day to mend.

To put together an on-the-go mending kit: Keep mending essentials in a little zippered or drawstring pouch so you can work on projects while out and about. The supplies you choose to take with you will depend on what project you are currently working on, but it can be helpful to keep these essentials in your kit just in case of an emergency (like a busted seam in your pants!): a few needles, a few pins, a few pieces of patch fabric, a safety pin or two, some thread, and a pair of scissors.

Here are some suggestions for keeping needles and pins organized in your mending kit:

- Attach them to a piece of felt or canvas.

- Keep them in a small tin (such as a tin for mints).

- Stick them to a small refrigerator magnet.

- Find a small pincushion to hold them.

To prevent sharp scissors (like embroidery scissors) from poking through your kit pouch, wrap the tip with a scrap of cloth and secure with a rubber band (or even sew a sheath for your scissors using heavy-duty fabric like denim, canvas, or thick felt).

Fabric Basics

Gaining basic fabric literacy is a crucial step in becoming a mender. By feeling the fabric, looking at its structure, and of course, reading the tag on a garment (when there is one), you will become adept at identifying the basic fabric types and when it is appropriate to use each.

Woven versus Knit

The two basic structures of fabric are woven and knit. You can often differentiate between the two just by looking at each closely and observing how the fabric is constructed.

Woven fabric is made of threads, called the warp and the weft, running perpendicular and *interlaced* with each other. Examples of common woven fabrics are denim, poplin (medium weight, usually for shirting), canvas, flannel, sheeting (for bedding), linen, and cotton quilting fabric.

Knit fabric is made of threads or yarn *interlooped* with each other. Examples of common knit fabrics are jersey (like T-shirt), sweatshirt, rib knit, sweater, and handknits, such as socks.

woven

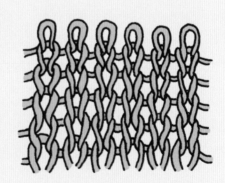

knit

Another way to determine whether a fabric is knit or woven is to stretch it in two directions: woven fabric will not stretch in either direction, while knits will stretch in at least one direction—and often both.

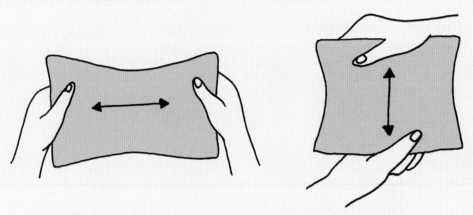

This difference in structure is one reason why choosing a patch fabric that matches the garment is important; a woven patch on a pair of stretchy knit leggings wouldn't feel comfortable and would tug on the leggings because of its rigidity, possibly creating more holes. Similarly, a knit patch on a pair of jeans would be too flimsy.

Synthetic versus Natural Fibers

Synthetic fibers are man-made, often petroleum based, and produced through intense chemical processes. Polyester, acrylic, and nylon are all examples of fabrics made of synthetic fibers. These materials are often inexpensive and highly durable, but they are a nightmare for the planet—their durability means they last forever in our landfills. Until more recently, synthetic fibers were reserved for activewear and outerwear, but now they are used in our everyday clothing (even socks and underwear). Dangerous to workers during production and to the consumer during repeated wears, synthetic garments like polyester fleeces degrade and shed microfibers (tiny fragments of plastic) into the air and into water every time they are machine washed.[1] Since these microfibers are too small to get caught in water treatment plants, they end up in our waterways and make up a significant portion of plastic waste entering the ocean. Microfibers have even been found in bottled water.[2]

Natural-fiber fabrics are better options for everyday clothing than synthetics. Natural fibers are plant or animal based, such as cotton, hemp, linen, silk, and wool. Bamboo has been marketed as a natural, environmentally friendly option, but it is in fact often produced through extremely chemically intensive processes. There are drawbacks to cotton and wool too, as cotton requires an immense amount of water to grow, and industrial-scale wool production has been exposed for animal cruelty in its treatment of sheep. Hemp is currently the most promising alternative, as it is incredibly durable, requires little fertilizer or water to grow, and self-seeds. The truth is that the global scale of production is rife with issues. One of the best things we can do is buy fewer new textiles.

+ + + + + + + + + + + + + + + + +

Note Is almost everything you own synthetic? You're not alone: more than 60 percent of clothing is made with synthetic fibers. They are tricky to avoid. But you can reduce shedding of microfibers from the garments you already own by washing them less often, and when you do, hand washing and line drying them. As you acquire new garments over time, you can replace synthetic garments with ones made from natural fibers. We've made a habit of looking at tags when we thrift-store shop— stumbling upon an affordable silk blouse or 100 percent wool sweater is a major score!

VISIBLE VERSUS (NEARLY) INVISIBLE MENDING

Whether a mend is intentionally visible or not is a personal preference. We often prefer visible mends in most instances because they showcase our handiwork and flaunt the ingenuity of repair. We choose mismatching yarn, differently patterned fabric, bright-colored thread, and add decorative stitching. We never want to miss an opportunity to add stories and intrigue and celebrate the beauty of imperfection! However, we think a mend at the crotch or seat of the pants is really best made invisible, as you don't want it to draw attention. Nearly invisible mending can be accomplished by choosing thread and patch fabric that closely match the garment and by making small, tidy stitches.

A Keen Eye

Paying close attention to our clothes is like watching the weather. Before a big storm hits, there is a buildup of signs: clouds gather, the sky turns dark, the wind picks up. These signs tell us what's coming, so we are able to prepare. Likewise, if we notice when our clothes are showing the early signs of wear—thinning spots in the fabric, loose buttons, stubborn zippers—we can fortify them before they deteriorate too much. Try making a habit of inspecting your clothes on a regular basis, such as on laundry day, and setting aside garments with these signs of wear for mending—often the washing machine can make small problems a whole lot bigger.

Mending is daunting when clothes have huge, gaping holes. The task may then seem too laborious to take on, and it becomes much more tempting to buy a replacement. But if we practice observing the state of our clothing regularly, we can stay ahead of full-on holes and long-lost buttons. In this way, it is much less of a burden to care for them. As the old saying goes, "A stitch in time saves nine."

Basic Mending Skills

Perhaps you've never picked up a needle and thread before. Not to worry! These, along with the basic stitches, are the building blocks that will equip you for virtually any hand-sewing project. Learning to sew is invaluable at any age. We remember our parents teaching us to hand-sew puppets when we were four! Once you feel comfortable with these basics, gift someone else, young or old, the knowledge of how to sew.

How to Thread a Needle

1 Pull out about an arm's length of thread from the spool. Anything longer than an arm's length will get tangled and drive you crazy! Anything shorter may feel more manageable, but you will find yourself needing to add thread more often, which can be tedious.

2 Cut the thread on an angle. This will make it easier to thread the needle.

3 (a) Pull the thread through the eye of the needle. If you only need a single thread for stitching, pull the thread about a third of its length through the needle and knot only the long end of the thread (see page 22 for how to tie a knot). Each time you sew with a single thread, you will shorten the loose end of the thread and free up more thread to stitch with. (b) If you need a double thread for stitching, align the two thread ends and knot them together.

4 When sewing, hold the needle at the eye so you have a grip on both the needle *and* the thread; this way, the thread won't keep slipping out when you pull it taut.

+ + + + + + + + + + + +

Note Double thread is stronger than single thread and therefore is used when stitching an important seam. A double thread will also make more visible stitches. A single thread is useful when you'd like nearly invisible stitches or when the thread is already bulky and strong enough as a single strand, such as button and craft, embroidery, or sashiko.

1

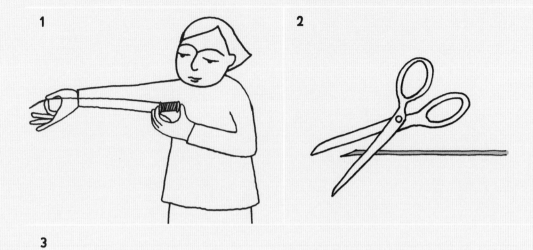

2

3

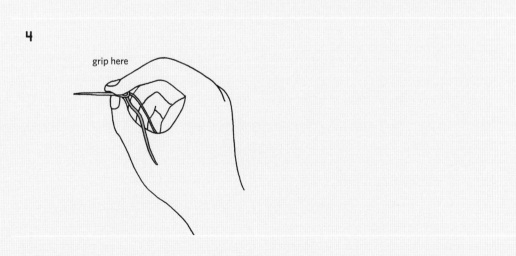

a   single thread

loose end   knot

b   double thread

knot

4

grip here

How to Tie an Overhand Knot

A knot at the end of your thread keeps the stitches from coming undone.

1 Loop the short tail end of the thread over the longer side.

2 (a) Bring the tail end through the loop. (b) The shape should look familiar—like a pretzel!

3 (a) As you are tightening the knot, you can position it at a desired point on the thread by holding the loose knot with your index finger and thumb and pulling the longer end with the other hand. (b) Tug on both ends of the thread to pull the knot small and tight.

4 Depending on how tight the weave of your fabric is, or how large of a needle you're using, one knot may not be big enough to keep the end from pulling through the fabric. Follow steps 1 through 3 to make a second knot, but when you are tightening it, go slowly so that you can position the loose second knot directly over the first. This may take a little bit of practice to align correctly.

WHEN TO USE A KNOT OR NOT

An overhand knot is useful to start sewing for most projects calling for all-purpose or button and craft thread. However, if you are mending with a bulky thread (like sashiko) or yarn, this knot will be too noticeable and uncomfortable when wearing the garment. This is particularly true for darning socks—a knot, no matter how tiny, may feel huge to a sensitive sole. Instead, sew a few stitches in place, on top of one another, to secure the thread or yarn (see page 26), and begin sewing.

1

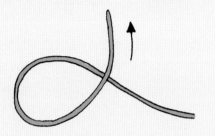

2a

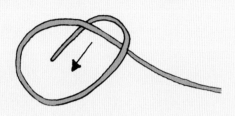

2b

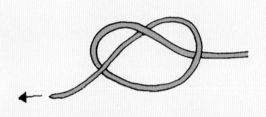

3a

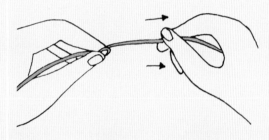

3b

4

Square Knot to Continue Sewing

While you always want to start with about an arm's length of thread for mending, you may run out before finishing a project. Obviously one way to continue sewing when you run out of thread is to tie off and replenish your needle with thread, but you can also use a handy square knot to continue sewing. The square knot will tie new thread to the remainder of your old thread. Because the square knot will leave two tails visible, this option works best when the underside of the fabric won't be seen.

1 When the thread has about 2 inches remaining, push the needle through to the underside of the fabric and slip it off the thread. Cut a new length of thread and thread the needle.

2 Hold the 2-inch tail in one hand and the end of the new thread in the other. Cross the tail end over the new thread end, aligning the thread at the base of the tail and against the fabric as close as possible.

3 Wrap the tail under the thread (just like when tying your shoes). Pull all three free threads taut so that this first "twist" is very close to the base of the thread tail.

4 Once again, cross the tail over the thread, this time in the opposite direction. Now the tail and thread are in the opposite hands.

5 Wrap the tail end *under* the thread.

6 Carefully pull all the threads taut so that the knot is again as close to the base of the tail as possible. Cut the two loose ends fairly close to the knot but be sure to leave at least a ¼-inch tail on each. Now you are ready to continue sewing!

+ +

Note A square knot is basically two "twists" of the threads on top of one another in opposite directions. There is a little saying I have to murmur under my breath every time I tie this knot, just so I can keep straight which thread goes over or under: "Left over right, right over left." This means if the left thread first crosses over (and wraps under) the right thread, then for the next twist, the right thread crosses over (and wraps under) the left thread. And the reverse is true too: if you start with the right crossed over the left, then it would be: "Right over left, left over right." —*Sonya*

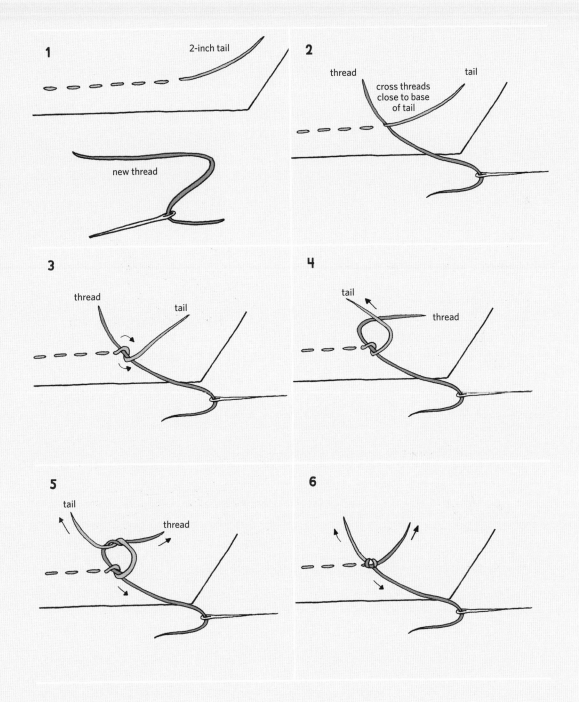

1 2-inch tail

new thread

2 thread tail

cross threads
close to base
of tail

3 thread tail

4 tail

thread

5 tail

thread

6

Stitch in Place to Finish Sewing

When you have come to the end of your sewing, you will need to tie off before the thread gets too short (when you have about 5 inches of thread remaining).

1 Sew one stitch in place. (Note that the illustration demonstrates a right-to-left sewing direction.)

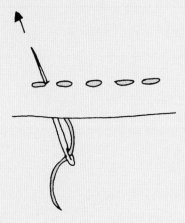

2 Sew a second stitch right on top of the first.

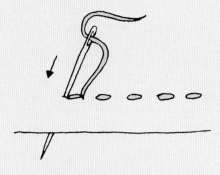

3 Sew a third stitch right on top of the first two, but before pulling the thread taut, push the needle through the loop in the thread. Pull the thread taut, locking the thread in place.

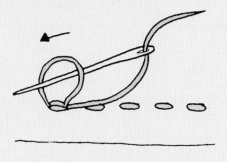

4 Finally, push the needle through to the underside of the project and cut the excess thread.

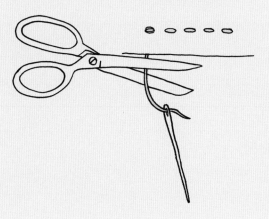

Basic Stitches

These are the stitches we use for hand mending, and they happen to be the most essential simple stitches you need to know for most hand-sewing projects. If you are a beginner, don't get too hung up on neatness—it will come with practice; the more you sew you will discover how to comfortably hold the fabric and the needle so that you have the most control.

Running Stitch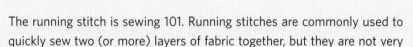

The running stitch is sewing 101. Running stitches are commonly used to quickly sew two (or more) layers of fabric together, but they are not very strong. In this book's projects, we recommend the running stitch primarily as a reinforcement stitch.

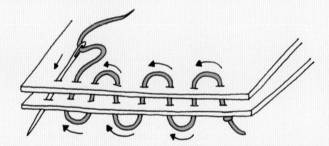

Strive for ¼-inch stitches that are spaced about ¼ inch apart. The trick to quick, even stitching is to take up multiple short stitches (three or four if your needle length allows) onto the needle before pulling the thread all the way through.

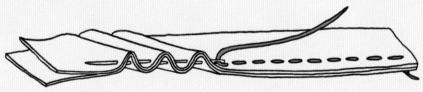

Whip Stitch

The whip stitch is fast, easy, and can be nearly invisible if you make tiny stitches and use thread that matches the fabric. The smaller and closer together these stitches are, the more securely two pieces of fabric will be attached. We call for this stitch most frequently to sew around the perimeter of a patch to attach it to a garment (though it makes other appearances as well). This stitch can be especially useful if you are sewing onto furniture where you can't access the underside of the fabric you are sewing the patch onto.

1 Thread a needle and knot the end. Insert the needle under the corner of the top layer of fabric. Ideally you should insert it no more than ⅛ inch from the edge of the fabric. The sewing direction will be from right to left.

2 Pull the needle and thread up through the top layer of fabric; the knot should be sandwiched snug between the two fabric layers.

3 Insert the needle into the bottom fabric directly below where the thread just came through, but before pulling the needle all the way through the fabric, angle the needle 45 degrees diagonally up and to the left to push it up through both layers of fabric about ⅛ to ¼ inch beside your first stitch. Now pull the needle and thread taut. This is your first whip stitch. Take care to keep stitches small and neat from here on out. Notice that the needle never disappears entirely below the bottom fabric—each stitch is made from the top side alone.

4 Once again, insert the needle into the bottom fabric directly below where the thread just came through, angling it to the left and pushing it up through both layers of fabric about ⅛ to ¼ inch to the left of your previous stitch. This is your second whip stitch.

5 Continue sewing, keeping the stitches close together, evenly spaced, and no more than ⅛ inch from the top fabric edge to make tidy little stitches all the way across.

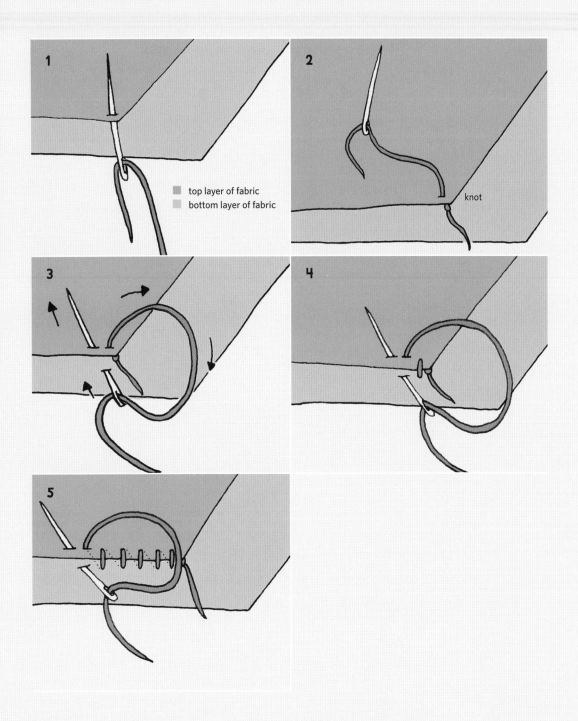

top layer of fabric
bottom layer of fabric

knot

Backstitch

A backstitch is often used to sew a very strong seam—it is essentially a beefed-up running stitch. The illustrations show sewing from right to left, so any stitch in that direction is advancing *forward*, while stitches going from left to right are moving *back*. When using a backstitch to sew a seam, it is best to leave at least a ¼-inch seam allowance.

1 Thread a needle and knot the end. Push the needle up through the underside of the fabric about ¼ inch ahead (to the left) of where you want the seam to actually begin. Pull the thread taut against the knot. The first stitch will be back—push the needle down through the fabric to the right of where you pulled the needle up.

2 Push the needle up through the underside of the fabric about ¼ inch ahead (to the left) of the first stitch and pull the thread taut.

3 The next stitch is again back—push the needle down through the fabric right beside where you pulled the needle up to begin the first stitch.

4 Again, push the needle up through the underside of the fabric about ¼ inch ahead (to the left) of the previous stitch and pull the thread taut. Notice the leapfrog pattern: after every stitch back, there is a stitch that leaps ahead.

5 Keep following this leapfrog pattern until you reach the end of your seam.

6 Pull the thread taut to tighten the stitches.

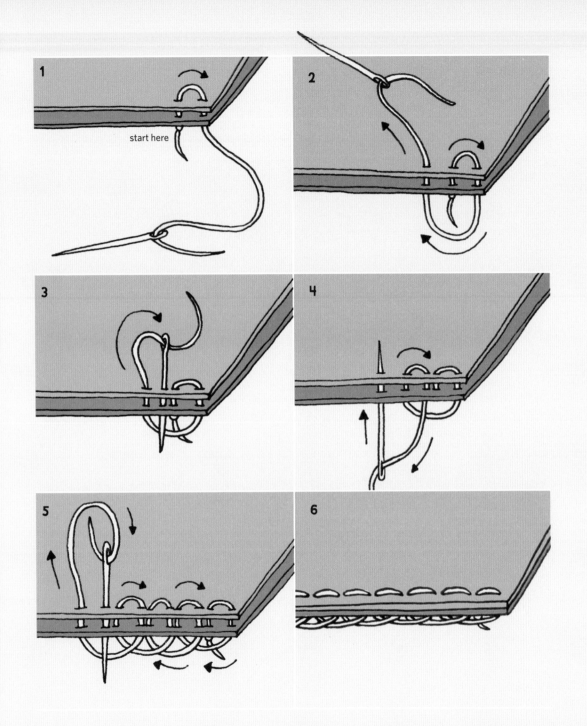

start here

Sashiko Stitching

Sashiko is a striking Japanese hand-sewing technique for reinforcement and decoration. Traditionally, white cotton thread was used to sew sashiko stitches on layers of indigo-dyed cotton, reworking the fabric into various usable forms, perhaps starting as a kimono, then remade into work clothes, then incorporated into a quilt, and finally rags. The evolving patchwork textiles, called *boro*, were a beautiful combination of different fabrics and stitches, accumulated over time, often reflecting multiple people's sewing contributions.

The sashiko technique requires a bit of planning and patience. We recommend using sashiko stitching over a patched area as reinforcement, but you may choose to apply this technique anywhere as an attractive embellishment. We have included instructions for four stitch designs of varying difficulty and time required.

Supplies

- Sashiko or embroidery needle: experiment with needle size; whichever one you choose will need an eye big enough to thread the rather bulky sashiko thread, but a smaller-weave fabric may need a smaller needle.

- Sashiko or embroidery thread

- Fabric pencil

- Ruler

- Scissors

MARKING

A grid can help you create a uniform stitch pattern. To draw a grid onto the area you will be stitching, use a fabric pencil and ruler. The grid size will depend on the total area and overall design, so see each tutorial for our recommendations. Before marking, lay the garment flat on a hard surface (and iron, if necessary) for best results.

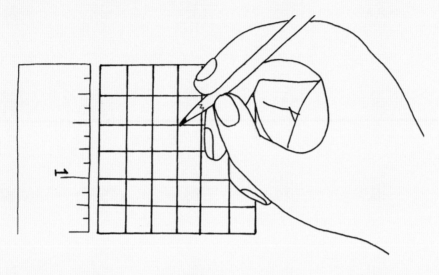

STITCH SIZE

Traditionally, sashiko stitches are very even and neat, which can be achieved by using this technique: instead of pushing the needle in and pulling the thread all the way through the fabric for each individual stitch, pick up multiple stitches on the needle at a time before pulling the thread. Be sure to keep the stitches fairly loose—after each pull of the thread, flatten out the fabric to prevent puckering. This technique can take practice to master, so be patient with yourself!

The stitch size will vary depending on the thickness of what you are sewing. Smaller stitches are easier to achieve on thinner material; thicker material (or multiple fabric layers) may only allow longer stitches. We like to aim for stitches around ⅛ to ⅜ inch long, depending on the fabric, but ultimately stitch size is your preference.

Rows of Running Stitches

This technique is the simplest, quickest way to reinforce a patch and add uniqueness to your mend, all while getting *lots* of practice sewing your running stitch. Remember how we said the running stitch is not strong? Well, *many* rows of running stitches are very strong! For details about how to sew a basic running stitch, see page 27. For running stitch inspiration, seek out stunning examples of the Japanese *boro* tradition and the *kantha* quilts of India.

1 If you'd like perfectly straight, even rows of stitching, draw only the horizontal lines of a grid onto the patch. We recommend grid lines that are either ¼ inch apart (for dense stitching) or ½ inch apart (for more spacious stitching). However, we also like the look of basic rows of running stitches sewn without a grid—they may not be precise, but we think they look charmingly imperfect.

2 Thread a needle with a single sashiko thread. Knot the end (see page 22). Begin the running stitch, sewing along the bottom edge of the patch.

3 When you reach the other side of the patch, change the sewing direction. To do this, push the needle down through the fabric at the left edge and pull the needle up through the fabric directly above your last row (if you have a grid marked

out, bring the needle up on the line above the stitches you just sewed). This vertical stitch will be hidden under the fabric (see illustration; the dotted line is the thread below the fabric). Sew the next row in the opposite direction of the first one. **Helpful hint:** When you get to the end of a row of stitches, you may find it easier to rotate your entire project so that you can stitch in the direction that feels most comfortable.

4 Again, when you reach the edge of the patch, push the needle down into the fabric and pull it up to start the next row to run parallel to the other two. Sew back in the other direction.

5 Continue in this way until the whole patch is covered in rows of running stitches.

6 When you complete all rows, stitch in place to finish sewing (see page 26).

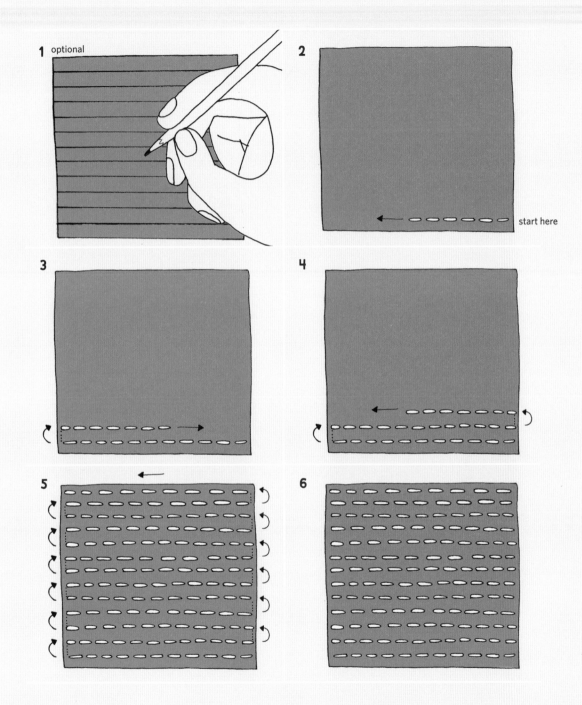

1 optional

2 start here

3

4

5

6

Little Pluses ✛ ✛ ✛ ✛ ✛ ✛ ✛ ✛

This simple stitch dots a patch with playful little plus marks while reinforcing a mend. It's also a great way to practice following a grid with both horizontal and vertical stitches.

1 Using a fabric pencil and a ruler, draw a grid on the fabric. The smaller the grid, the closer together the pluses will be. We recommend a ½-inch grid for this design; a smaller one will make keeping space between the stitches a challenge, while a larger grid will space them out too much.

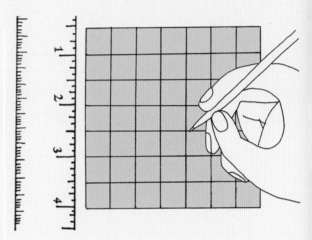

2 Thread a needle with a single sashiko thread and knot the end (see page 22). Starting in the bottom right corner, sew a running stitch along the bottom edge of the patch, from right to left, using the first horizontal line of the grid as your guide. Center each stitch at the intersection of the grid lines. Strive to make the space between stitches one third of the stitch length.

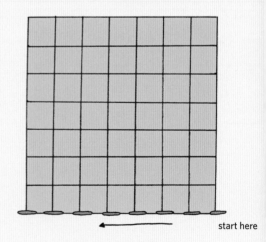

start here

3 At the end of the first row, push the needle down through the fabric and pull it back up at the start of the next horizontal row above (see illustration; the dotted line is the thread below the fabric). Sew this next row of running stitches from left to right in the same manner as the first row. **Helpful hint:** When you get to the end of the row of stitches, you may find it easier to rotate your entire project so that you can stitch in the direction that feels most comfortable.

4 At the end of the second row of stitching, again push the needle down through the fabric and up at the start of the third row, sewing from right to left to complete the third row of stitches.

5 Continue sewing horizontal rows until the grid is full.

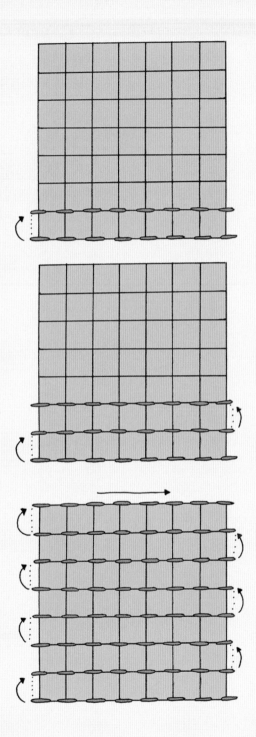

6 At the end of the last horizontal row, push the needle down through the fabric and pull it back up on the vertical line that crosses it. Stitch a vertical row of running stitches, from top to bottom, so that each stitch crosses the horizontal stitches where the grid lines intersect.

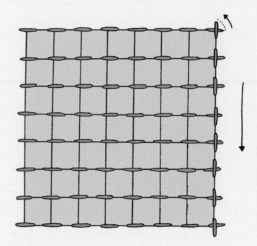

7 Continue with the next vertical row. Working from bottom to top, sew vertical running stitches that cross the horizontal stitches.

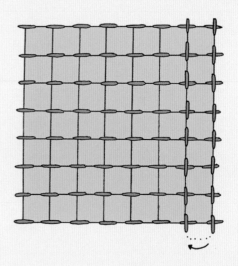

8 Cross all remaining stitches in this manner.

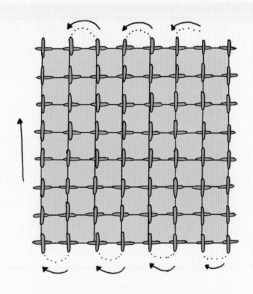

9 At the end of the last vertical row, stitch in place to finish sewing (see page 26).

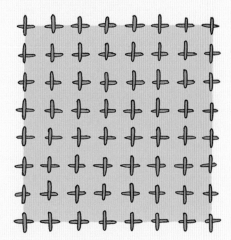

Stars ✳ ✳ ✳ ✳ ✳ ✳

This sweet design simply builds on Little Pluses (page 36). It is a bit more time consuming because you are sewing back over each plus sign two additional times diagonally, but the result is striking!

1 To make stars, complete the Little Pluses instructions through step 8. When you get to the final corner, don't stitch in place—instead, keep sewing by crossing back diagonally over the last plus sign (see illustration; the dotted line is the thread below the fabric).

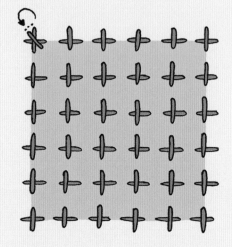

2 Make the next stitch over the plus below the last, with the diagonal going the opposite direction of the first stitch. Continue in this manner until you reach the bottom of the vertical row.

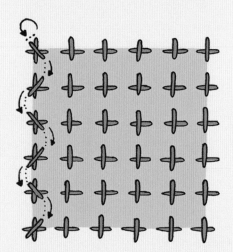

3 Then, in that same row, cross the thread under the bottom plus sign and stitch diagonally in the opposite direction of the previous stitch.

4 Continue upward, diagonally crossing each star in the first row.

5 (a) Once you've completed one row of stars, move on to the next row, sewing diagonal stitches from top to bottom.

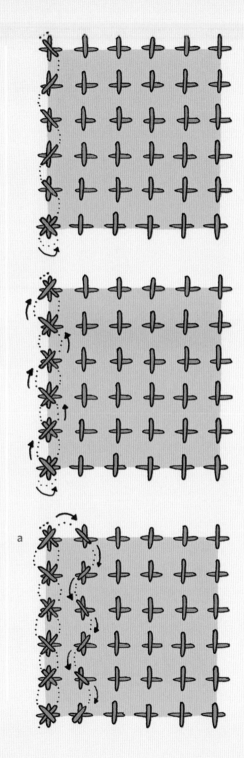

5 (b) Then sew diagonal stitches from bottom to top.

6 Continue sewing, crossing each row of pluses twice to make stars.

7 At the end of the last vertical row, stitch in place to finish sewing (see page 26).

Open Flowers

This design looks like little flowers (or fireworks!) bursting open. Its overall effect is a bit more delicate than Stars, but it is also more complicated and time consuming to execute: each flower is composed of twice as many stitches, and it looks best if the stitches are small.

+ +

Note For success with this design, especially when patching or doing other projects involving more than one layer or heavier-weight fabrics, we recommend bringing the needle and thread through the fabric completely with each stitch instead of gathering many stitches onto the needle.

1 Using a fabric pencil and a ruler, draw a grid on the fabric, as shown in the illustration. This design should have a grid with ½- to ¾-inch squares.

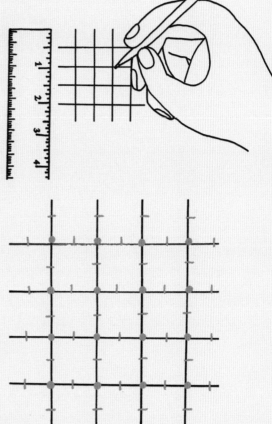

2 It can be helpful to draw (or imagine) small tick marks halfway between the grid-line intersections, as well as small dots at each intersection. As you sew running stitches, you will pass *under* each dot and midway tick mark.

3 Thread a needle with a single sashiko thread and knot the end. Starting in the bottom right corner, begin the running stitches, sewing from right to left along the first grid line. Be sure to push the needle *under* each dot at the grid intersections and *under* each tick mark halfway between.

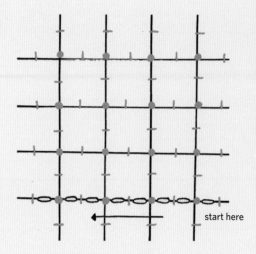

start here

4 When you reach the end of the first row, push the needle down through the fabric and pull it back up at the start of the next horizontal row above. This vertical stitch will be hidden under the fabric (see illustration; the dotted lines are the thread below the fabric). Sew the next row of running stitches from left to right in the same manner as the first. When you reach the end of the second row, push the needle down through the fabric and up again to start the third row; continue stitching the third row from right to left. **Helpful hint:** When you get to the end of the row of stitches, you may find it easier to rotate your entire project so that you can stitch in the direction that feels most comfortable.

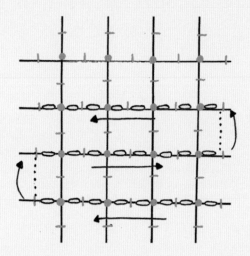

5 Keep sewing in this manner, back and forth, until you reach the final row. At the corner of the final row, stitch vertically down and under each horizontal row. Remember to stitch under the intersections and the halfway tick marks.

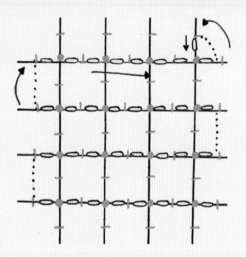

6 Continue sewing the vertical rows of stitches from top to bottom and bottom to top until the grid is full of open plus signs.

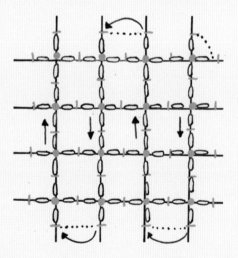

7 When you finish the final row, turn the corner by pulling the needle and thread up between the two corner stitches. Stitch diagonally toward the center of the flower, being sure to stitch under the grid intersection. Continue diagonally down the first row, alternating the direction of the stitch for each flower.

8 When you reach the bottom of the vertical row, cross the thread under the bottom flower and stitch diagonally in the opposite direction of the previous stitch, working your way back up to the top of the row.

9 On your final diagonal stitch of this first row, push the needle down through the fabric and pull it up between the two corner stitches of the second vertical row. Continue stitching diagonally down the row.

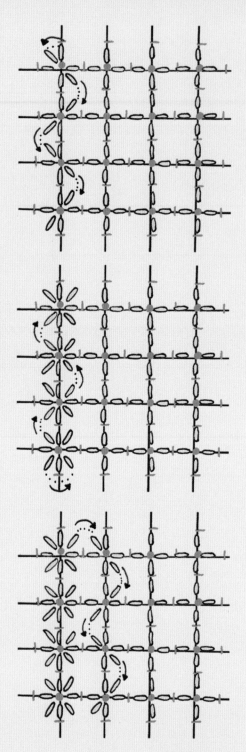

10 Proceed in this manner, working your way up and down each vertical row and making opposite diagonal stitches until the grid is complete.

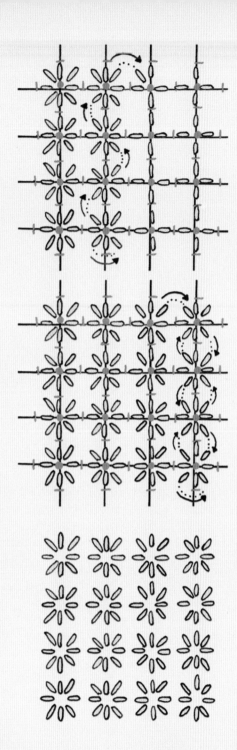

11 At the end of the last vertical row, stitch in place to finish sewing (see page 26). The illustration shows what the finished design should look like.

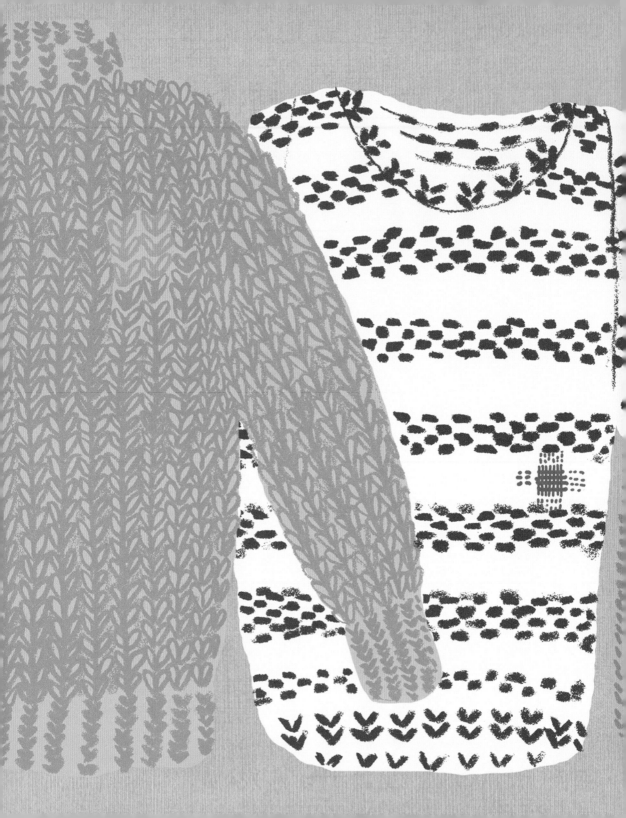

Darning

A friend tells me about her favorite sweater and how she's afraid if the holes get any bigger, it will be a lost cause. She says, "It has been with me through so much—at first I didn't quite like it, but something kept me from giving it away. Each time I rediscovered it hidden at the bottom of my dresser drawer, it would call to me softly, but I would always reach for another, more familiar sweater. Later I found it tucked deep in my moving boxes. In my new place, it hung neglected in the back of the closet, the shoulders distended from spending so much uninterrupted time on a hanger.

"One day, for some reason, I reached for it and put it on, just to see. I was getting ready for my big bike trip, and it turned out to be the best warm thing as I crossed the country. It has suffered snags and snares, mud splats and dribbled food, rainstorms and sweaty pits. Now it's the only thing that goes well over my favorite shirt. In the fall, I wear it nearly every day. So . . . we can't part ways now."

I offer to fix it. She's skeptical: "It's really pretty far gone," she says—she can feel the breeze blowing through the tatters. I examine the damage; there are little holes everywhere, congregating at the bottom hem, peppering the sleeves, threatening to disconnect the neckline from the rest of the sweater. And the elbows are, of course, gaping holes. "I can fix it," I reassure her. "Okay," she finally says.

At home, I gather what I need and sit with her sweater draped over my lap, warming me. I choose a hole to start on, pick a colorful scrap of yarn, and begin the process of loving this thing she loves so much. I am breathing new life into it so it can go on keeping her warm. And in doing so, I am adding to the story this sweater already tells, the story my friend will proudly share as she wears it for, hopefully, many more years to come. She'll say, "This sweater was brought back from the dead by my dear friend; she's a wizard all right."

—Sonya

The Art of Darning

Darning a hole is surprisingly simple. Essentially you are re-creating fabric to fill a hole or reinforce fabric where it is wearing thin. Plain weave darning is our go-to technique for filling a hole in a knitted garment, but there are several useful alternatives that we will cover in this section as well: a crocheted patch, a knitted patch, and a needle-felted patch (which doesn't use yarn at all!). A threadbare spot can be beautifully reconstructed with Swiss darning (often called duplicate stitch). These techniques can be used on all sorts of knitted garments and textiles: sweaters, socks, hats, gloves, blankets, and more.

Choosing the Right Needle

We like to use a tapestry needle to darn because it is blunt and has a big eye for threading yarn. If your chosen yarn is somewhat thick, use a large needle with a big eye; if the yarn is thin, a smaller needle will suffice. A darning needle can be used as an alternative.

Choosing the Right Yarn

It is important to choose the right yarn for each darning project—try to match the approximate thickness of the garment's original yarn. As a rule of thumb, when choosing yarn for darning socks, it's better to err on the lighter, thinner side than the thicker, bulkier side so that you don't feel a bulky mend when wearing them. For a sweater, it is better to pick a slightly thicker yarn than the sweater's so that the mend isn't too "airy." However, if you do choose a thin yarn for a bulkier garment, you can double the yarn to avoid this.

We also recommend trying to match the type of fiber your garment is woven with. In other words, if the garment is made of merino wool, try to darn the garment with wool yarn. This way, the garment can be treated as one material when you wash it.

Of course, it can be hard to match the exact color, thickness, and material of a garment's yarn—this is an opportunity to get creative! You can choose to highlight your mend by using a contrasting colored yarn, or experiment with a different-textured yarn than the one the garment was made with. For garments that are knit with very thin yarn, use sock weight yarn, wool darning thread, or embroidery thread for darning. Embroidery thread can even be divided further into just a few threads for mending very small holes or delicate materials.

Before You Begin

These essential techniques will help you start and finish your project.

THREADING THE NEEDLE
Here is a trick for threading yarn onto a tapestry needle: fold the end of the yarn and push the folded end through the eye of the needle. This way, you aren't battling loose and unraveling fibers!

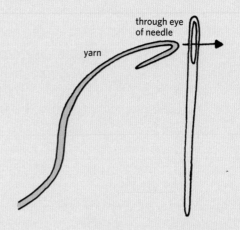

yarn

through eye of needle

SECURING THE YARN TO BEGIN

1 There are no knots in darning! A knot at the end of the yarn would be noticeable and perhaps irritating, especially in socks. Instead, begin darning by pushing the needle up through the underside of the fabric, about ½ inch from the edge of the hole. Pull the yarn through, leaving about a 4-inch tail on the underside. (You will come back to weave this in later.)

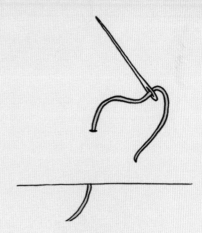

2 Stitch in place once.

3 Stitch again on top of the first stitch to secure the yarn to the fabric and begin your work.

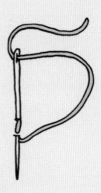

TYING OFF THE YARN

When you are finished with your darn (or if you need to replenish your yarn partway through a project), follow these steps.

1 Insert the needle into an existing stitch at the edge of the completed stitching, but don't pull the yarn through completely.

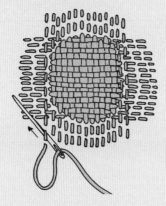

2 Thread the needle through the loop of yarn and then pull tight. This secures the yarn in place.

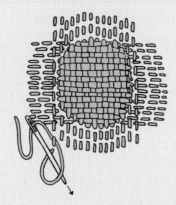

3 Sew three or four running stitches alongside your work to weave in the tail, ending with the needle on the underside of the fabric. Cut close

to the last stitch so no tail is visible. If you are darning a bulky garment, these stitches do not need to be deep (or go all the way through to the other side)—they can be shallow as long as the thread is woven under *some* yarn.

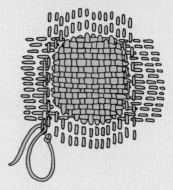

4 Turn the garment inside out, thread the tapestry needle onto any tails, and sew a few running stitches alongside the darn to weave them in. Oftentimes, if you are using wool yarn to darn a wool sock, the repeated friction of wearing and washing the sock will actually *felt together* the darning yarns and further lock the stitches and tail ends in place.

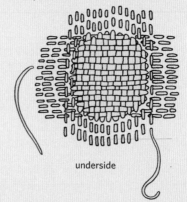

underside

Mending Life

Plain Weave Darning

Simple and versatile, plain weave darning is the perfect technique for fixing small holes such as those from moths, burns, and minor tears. Bigger holes can also be mended with the plain weave darn, but the bigger the hole, the more challenging it is to neatly fill. Plain weave darning can be carried out on any knitted item such as a sweater, blanket, scarf, or hat. To mend with this technique on a sock or glove, it's easiest to use a darning tool (see page 11). Be aware that plain weave darning is not stretchy, and though it will fill a hole in a sock, the mend will not give like the surrounding knit.

Supplies

- Tapestry needle

- Yarn (see recommendations on how to choose yarn on page 53)

- Scissors

- Darning tool (if mending socks or gloves)

- Embroidery hoop (optional, see page 11 for when to use a hoop)

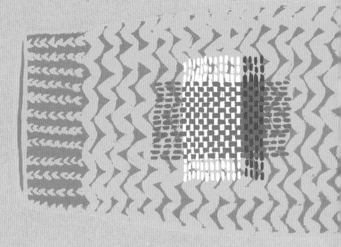

Remember, there are many good ways to mend, and mending is an adventure! Plain weave darning is an excellent way to mend small holes and threadbare spots in woven fabrics too. Experiment on dresses, shirts, tablecloths, and other linens using colorful sashiko or embroidery thread and a medium needle.

1 Clean up the hole by cutting away any ragged edges and loose yarn ends.

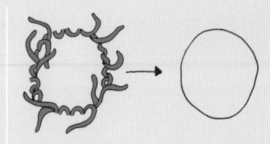

2 Thread a tapestry needle with a single yarn (unless you are doubling it to mimic a thicker yarn). Again, as a general rule of thumb, it's helpful to use a piece of yarn no longer than arm's length to prevent tangling.

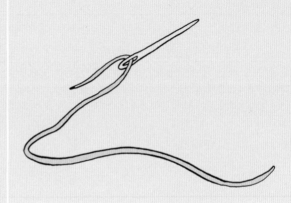

3 If you're using an embroidery hoop, stretch the fabric over the hoop with the top side of the fabric facing up. The hole should be isolated in the center of the hoop. Do not stretch the fabric beyond its natural give—just enough to keep it taut, like the top of a drum, but not distorting the hole. Clasp the hoop.

embroidery hoop

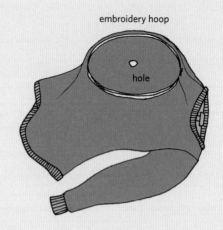

hole

Mending Life

4 Push the needle up through the underside of the fabric about ½ inch from the edge of the hole. Starting away from the edge of the hole ensures that the yarn is integrated into still-intact, well-structured fabric. Pull the yarn through, leaving about a 4-inch tail of yarn on the underside. Stitch in place twice to secure the yarn to the fabric. You will come back to weave the tail in later.

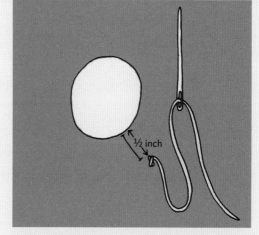

5 Begin a vertical running stitch.

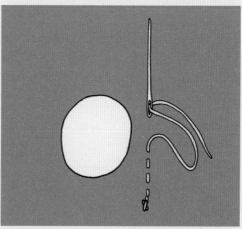

6 When you have sewn past the hole by about ½ inch (or more as preferred), reverse direction and sew running stitches down snug alongside the finished first row. To change direction: on your last stitch of the row, dip into the fabric as usual, but come up directly to the left, with the needle perpendicular to the finished row, where you will begin the next row of stitches. Changing direction this way will allow horizontal end stitches to be hidden on the back side of the fabric.

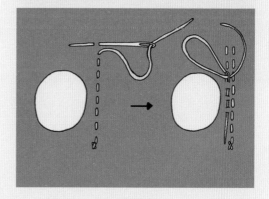

7 Stagger the stitches approaching the hole. When you reach the hole, gently pull yarn across it so that it spans the hole, and then continue the running stitch on the opposite side. Keep vertical rows close together, with no gap between them.

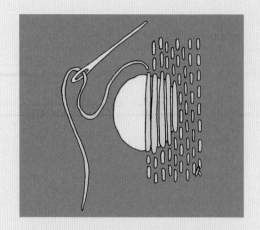

Note Take care not to pull the yarn too tight! If the yarn is pulled too taut, the finished mend will pucker. That said, try not to allow the yarn to be too loose either, or the darn will be distended. Finding the right tension can be difficult. It takes a bit of practice to get a feel for it, but if you go slow and check to make sure the fabric and yarns are lying flat within the hoop, you should be able to make a very tidy darn.

8 Continue stitching and spanning the hole until it is filled with tightly packed vertical yarns. For full coverage and security, continue sewing to the left of the hole by a few rows in the same way you began.

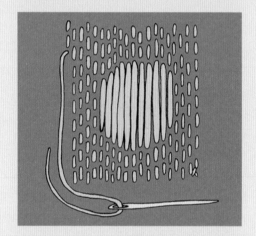

9 At this point, if you have plenty of yarn remaining on your needle, continue on with the horizontal stitches. If you need to replenish your yarn—or if you'd like to change color for an interesting effect—tie off the yarn (see page 56) and thread a new one.

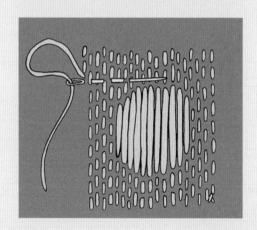

Mending Life

10 Begin weaving the yarn horizontally over and under the vertical stitches. As with the vertical stitches, sew beyond the edge of the hole to include the surrounding intact fabric, keeping the horizontal rows close together. The interwoven yarns should fully fill the hole.

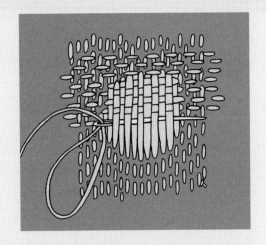

11 Pull the yarn through to the underside of the fabric. Tie off the yarn and weave in any remaining tails (see page 56).

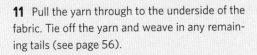

Note If you finish a darn and you notice that the weave is too "airy" (it's too "airy" if you can see through it), keep sewing back and forth to make the weave denser.

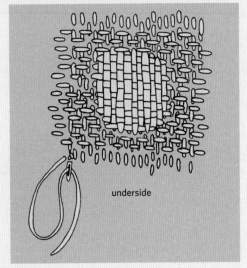

underside

For Socks

If you notice that you wear all your socks out in the same spot (such as the heel or back of the ankle), it's worth inspecting the inside of your shoes for torn lining where plastic or stiff leather is exposed and rubbing holes into your socks. If this is the case, take your shoes to a cobbler to mend the lining.

1 Clean up the hole by cutting away any ragged edges and loose yarn ends.

2 Thread a tapestry needle with a single yarn. A small hole will likely only require a foot of yarn, while a bigger hole might require 2 feet or more.

3 Push the needle up from the inside of the sock about ½ inch from the edge of the hole, leaving about a 3-inch tail of yarn on the underside. You don't need to come back to weave in the tail at the end of the project because it will be hidden on the inside of the sock. Stitch in place twice to attach the yarn to the sock.

4 Insert the darning tool into the sock, situating it under the hole. Gather the sock around the "neck" of the tool but not too tightly, so the hole doesn't get distorted. If you're using a tool without a neck, such as a darning egg or an orange, just gather the sock together at the base of the tool.

5 Follow steps 5 through 10 of the Plain Weave Darning tutorial on page 59 through 61. End your last stitch on the inside of the sock. There's no need to weave in loose tails inside the sock—over time they will felt together with the sock!

+ +

Note When we first learned to darn our socks, it was a game-changer. No longer did a hole in a sock mean it was rendered useless. No longer did we have to wonder what the heck to do with holey socks when we couldn't bring ourselves to toss them but certainly couldn't donate them. You can use this technique, or Swiss Darning on page 68, to mend your store-bought, machine-knitted socks too. However, you may find that in machine-knitted socks the yarn weight is so delicate and the stitch size so small that it doesn't really look like knitting at all. If this is the case, try using a thinner yarn such as sock weight or even embroidery thread with a small tapestry needle (or large embroidery needle). If you are Swiss darning on a sock with stitches that are too small to accurately duplicate, don't worry about following the existing stitches perfectly! Instead, sew the duplicate stitches to generally cover the threadbare area, which will reinforce it.

1

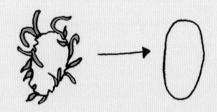

2

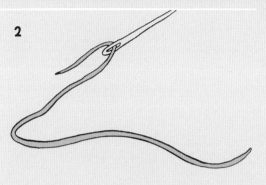

3

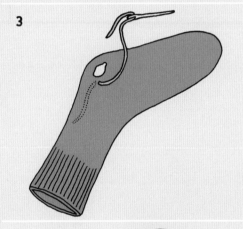

4

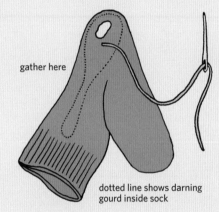

gather here

dotted line shows darning
gourd inside sock

5

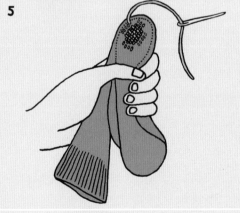

It's just a sock
A fifty-cent sock
A holey sock
A bunchy sock
A sock like so many other socks

But

It's not just a sock
It's rain and soil
Sunshine and wind
It's hard work and
Long distances
Sleepless nights and
Missed meals

But

It's just a sock
A broken sock
When everyone shouts
Why bother? It's not worth it

I keep sewing

For Gloves

To darn a glove finger with the plain weave darning technique, you'll want to work with a darning tool to keep the natural shape of the finger. If you have a darning mushroom or gourd, often the handle works well inserted into the finger of the glove. The fat end of a carrot or the handle of a kitchen tool might do the trick as well. Take care to choose the appropriate needle size and thickness of yarn for your glove.

1 Clean up the hole by cutting away any ragged edges and loose yarn ends.

2 Thread a tapestry needle with a single yarn. A small hole will likely only require a foot of yarn, while a bigger hole might require 2 feet or more.

3 Push the needle up through the inside of the glove finger about ¼ inch from the edge of the hole, leaving about a 2-inch tail of yarn on the underside. You don't need to come back to weave in the tail at the end of the project because it will be hidden on the inside of the glove. Stitch in place twice to attach the yarn to the glove.

4 Insert the darning tool into the glove. Gather the glove around the tool but not too tightly, so the hole doesn't get distorted.

5 Follow steps 5 through 10 of the Plain Weave Darning tutorial on page 59 through 61. End your last stitch on the inside of the glove. There's no need to weave in loose tails inside the glove—over time they will felt together with the glove!

1

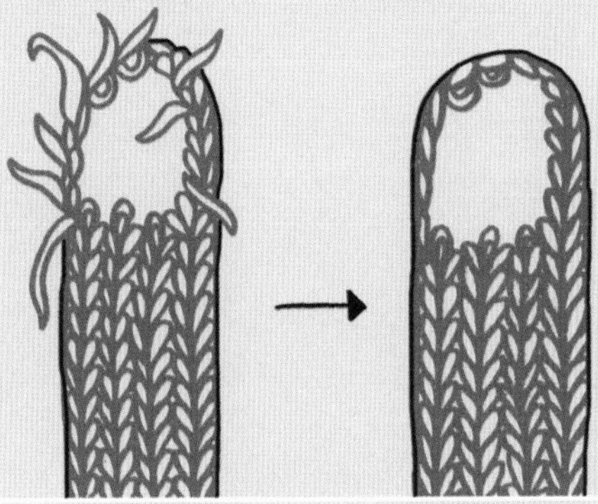

2

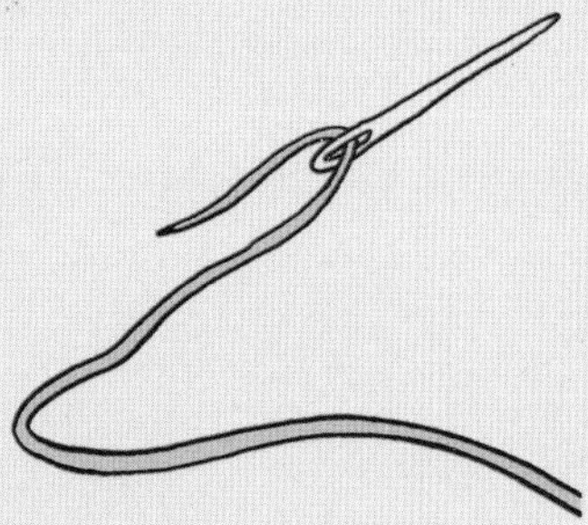

3

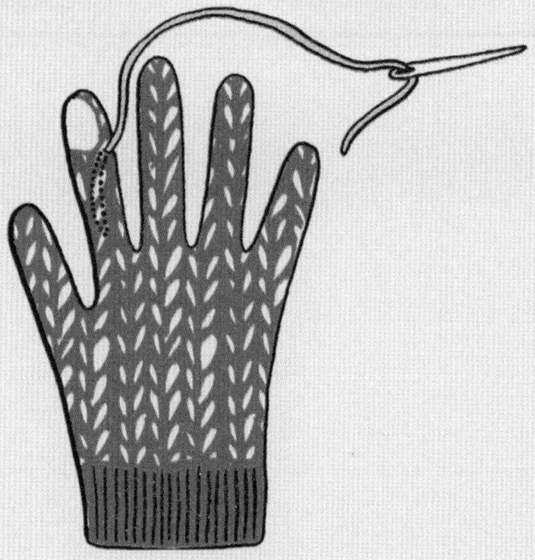

4

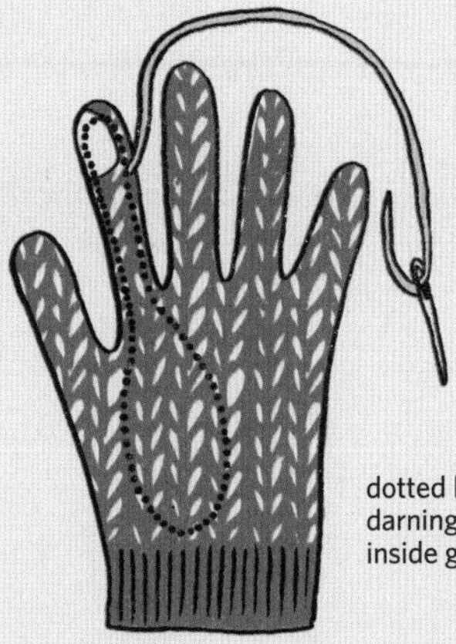

dotted line shows
darning gourd
inside glove

5

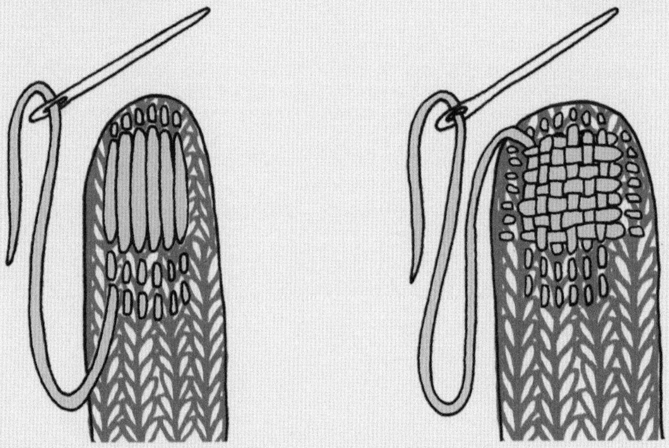

Swiss Darning (Also Known as Duplicate Stitch)

We recommend this proactive stitching technique for reinforcing an intact but threadbare area of a knit. With it, you are literally duplicating the existing yarn's path to help keep together a spot that's at risk of turning into a hole. This technique is usually done on a garment knitted in stockinette (a basic knitting stitch of alternating knit and purl rows) because it is the easiest knit to see and follow the stitches, or Vs, as we'll call them in this tutorial. In this tutorial, the blue is for the completed duplicate stitches, yellow is for the stitch you are working on duplicating, and pink is for the stitch above the one you're working on. Use a yarn that is the same weight as or thicker than the garment's yarn so that the duplicate stitches really fill in the gaps of the threadbare spot. This mending technique can be nearly invisible if you use the same colored yarn. Because the yarn is fully integrated into the fabric, it isn't bulky and it retains stretch—perfect for a sock or elbow mend. This mend is so seamless, it's totally brag-worthy!

Supplies

- Tapestry needle

- Yarn, the same weight as or slightly thicker than the garment's yarn

- Darning tool (if mending socks or gloves)

- Scissors

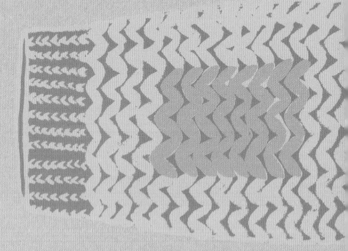

1 Take a look at your knit garment—notice that each stitch is a V. In the threadbare area (colored light green), the stitches will likely be thin, spread out, and may look less like Vs and more like inter-locking loops. The first stitch you will duplicate is the V (colored yellow) to the right and one row below the threadbare area. This ensures your reinforcement also integrates some fabric that is still in good shape. Sewing direction will be right to left for this first row.

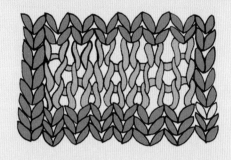

2 Push the needle up from the underside of the fabric at the base of this first V (yellow) and pull the yarn, leaving a 4-inch tail on the underside of the garment (you will come back to weave in this tail later).

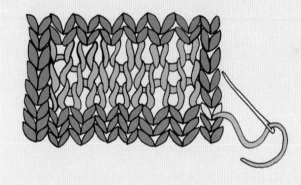

3 Cross the needle behind the pink V, which is just above the V you are duplicating (yellow).

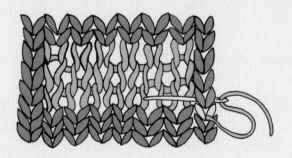

4 Insert the needle back into the base of the first V—this is where you began. This completes your first duplicate stitch (now blue).

5 Push the needle up from the underside of the fabric at the base of the second V (yellow), just to the left of the first V (blue).

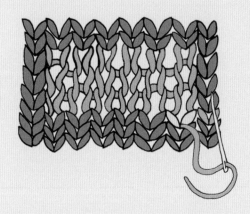

6 Cross the needle behind the pink V that is just above the V you are duplicating (yellow).

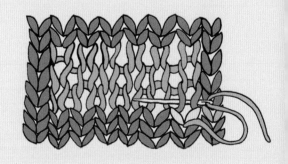

7 Insert the needle back into the base of the yellow V—this completes another duplicate stitch (now blue).

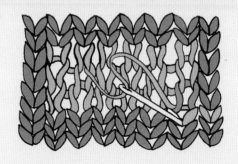

8 Continue sewing along the row of Vs in this manner, including and ending with the next intact stitch beyond the threadbare area. You will now start duplicating the stitches in the row above, sewing from left to right.

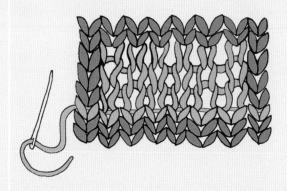

9 Push the needle up from the underside of the fabric at the base of the V (yellow) just *above* the last V you duplicated (blue).

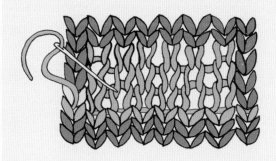

10 Cross the needle behind the pink V just above the V you are duplicating (yellow).

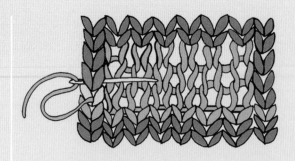

11 Insert the needle back into the base of the yellow V—this completes another duplicate stitch (now blue).

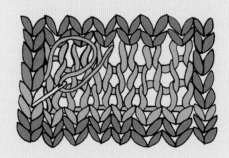

12 The next stitch you will duplicate is to the right (yellow). Follow the same pattern as before to duplicate this stitch: push the needle up from the underside of the fabric at the base of the yellow V, which is just to the right of the last V you duplicated. Cross the needle behind the pink V just above the V you are duplicating (yellow).

13 Insert the needle back into the base of the V (yellow)—this completes another duplicate stitch (now blue).

14 Duplicate the stitches all across this row in this same manner. When you reach the end of the row, cross the needle behind the pink V, which is just above the V you are duplicating (yellow). You will be stitching from right to left.

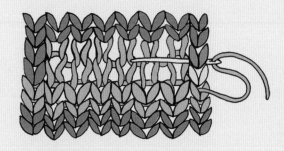

15 Continue sewing until the entire thread-bare area (and adjacent perimeter stitches) are duplicated. At your last stitch, push the needle through to the underside of the garment, tie off, and weave in any loose tails (see page 56).

a wish for well-being

Many people believe that handmade and mended items are infused with the love and care the maker or mender put into the object. In Korea, there is a beautiful textile tradition known as *jogakbo*. Small scraps of cloth are pieced together in an irregular, improvisational way, and the resulting patchwork wrap (known as *bojagi*) is used to carry everything from food to clothing. Given as gifts, the cloth wraps are believed to bring good luck because while making jogakbo, the sewer wishes for the recipient's good fortune and well-being. In the same way that *metta* meditation (the Buddhist practice of sending loving-kindness to all beings through a series of mantras) benefits the meditator as well as those around her, the effects of jogakbo on the person sewing are powerful.

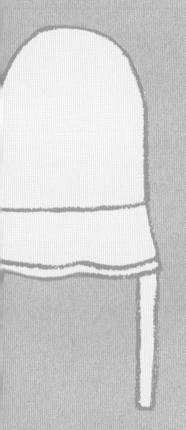

Crocheted Patch

One of the main reasons people throw a knitted garment away is because they're daunted by an area littered with little holes or a huge, misshapen hole, often in the elbows. The garment seems beyond rescue. But it's not too far gone! Instead, it is the perfect candidate for a beautiful circular crocheted patch. If you already know how to crochet, you're in luck—this is a perfect place to apply your skill. If you don't know how to crochet but want to give it a try, begin by seeking out one of the many tutorials available online, or find a friend who can teach you the basic crochet stitches.

Supplies

- Crochet hooks: small (3 mm) and large (5 mm)

- Yarn, matching the thickness of the garment's yarn

- Tapestry needle

- Scissors

- Iron (optional)

1 Clean up the hole by cutting away any ragged edges and loose yarn ends. If there is a cluster of small holes or runs, cut out the entire damaged area so that you are starting with a single, neat hole.

2 Make a slip knot in the yarn, loop it around the small crochet hook, and insert the hook into a spot on the hole's perimeter that is not too close to the edge—you want to be sure as you crochet around the hole that the stitches are grabbing stable fabric. Start with a single crochet stitch.

3 Continue to crochet around the perimeter of the hole with single crochet stitches, inserting the hook into the knitted fabric to anchor each stitch. Be sure to keep the stitches close together but slightly loose so as not to create any puckers in the garment.

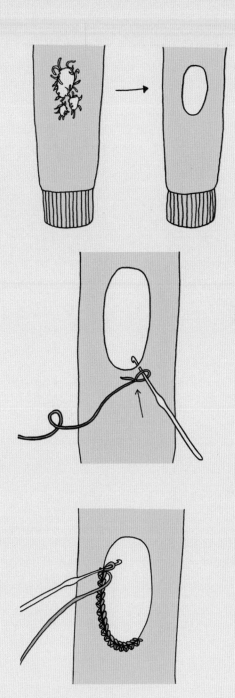

Darning

4 This first row of stitches should nicely bind the raw edge of the hole. When you reach the place where you started, connect the first and last stitch with a slip stitch. To more quickly fill in the hole, switch to the larger crochet hook.

5 Continue to crochet around the perimeter of the hole, decreasing stitches as you go to shorten each circle as they spiral toward the center. The frequency of decreased stitches will depend on the yarn you use and how loose the stitches are— see what works best for your mend. The closer you get to the center of the patch, the more frequently you will need to decrease stitches. There will be a balance to strike between snug stitches and keeping things loose enough to prevent puckering. The goal is a flat crocheted patch.

6 When the hole is completely filled, you will finish at the center of the patch. Thread the yarn onto a tapestry needle. Push the needle and yarn through to the underside of the patch (the inside of the garment). Tie off and weave in the tail (see page 56). Iron flat if needed.

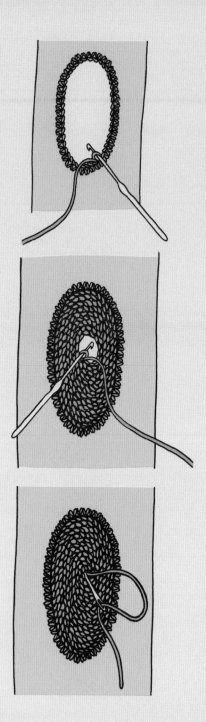

Knitted Patch

A knitted patch lies on top of the garment and can be a bit bulky, so it makes for a particularly good elbow patch, but some may feel it's not the best for a sock heel, toe, or sole (though plenty of socks are mended this way anyway!). If you already know how to knit, this method of patching a hole is a breeze—you essentially knit a swatch and secure it to the garment over the hole with whip stitches. If you don't know how to knit, there are many good books on the topic, as well as tutorials online.

While you certainly can try to match the patch yarn to the garment's, it is also fine to use scrap yarn that may not be perfectly coordinated. This will make the patch stand out—whether it be because of a different yarn thickness, color, or type of stitches—and that's the fun part of this mending method.

Supplies

- Yarn
- Knitting needles
- Tapestry needle
- Scissors
- Ruler

1 Experiment with how many stitches are needed to knit a patch that is approximately ½ inch wider than the hole by casting on your best guess and knitting a few rows. If this patch isn't wide enough or is too wide, take out the stitches and start over, casting on more or less. When you determine the right number of stitches, knit a patch approximately ½ inch taller than the height of the hole. Cast off.

2 Center the knitted patch over the hole.

3 Thread a tapestry needle with a single yarn, the same yarn as the knitted patch. Push the needle up through the underside of the garment at one corner of the patch, leaving about a 4-inch tail of yarn on the underside (you will come back to weave this in later). Secure the yarn to begin.

4 Whip stitch (see page 28) around the perimeter of the patch, sewing the patch onto the garment.

5 (a) When you reach the place where you began, stitch in place to secure the yarn (see page 26). Continue to sew a few running stitches toward the hole. (b) Continue to sew around the perimeter of the hole to secure the two layers of fabric together. Tie off and weave in the tail (see page 56).

1

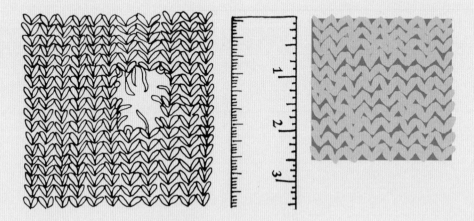

2

3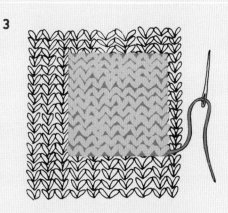

4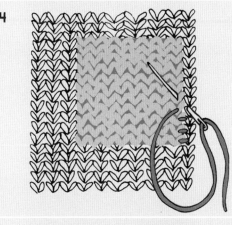

5a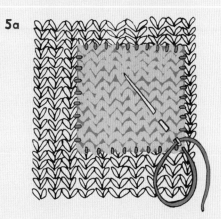

5b

Needle-Felted Patch

Needle-felting is a quick and easy way to fill a hole in a knitted or boiled wool garment (like a pea coat)—no sewing required! The magic is in how the special felting needle intertwines wool roving with the garment fibers: the barbs on the needle grab and tangle the two, enmeshing them together. You may never darn a sweater again after trying this—the result is a cute, colorful fuzzy patch in place of the hole (and some released aggression at the same time!).

Supplies

- Felting needle

- Rolled-up towel to fit inside the garment

- Scissors

- Wool roving

- Cookie cutter bigger than the hole that needs mending (optional)

1 Clean up the hole by cutting away any ragged edges and loose yarn ends.

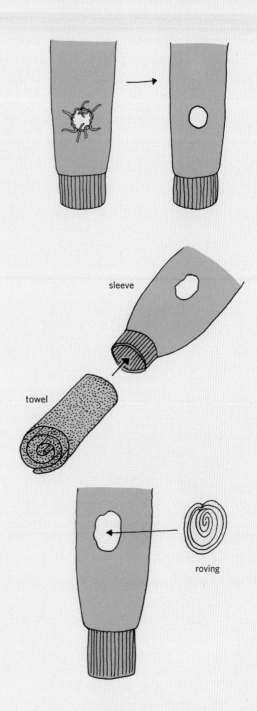

2 Place the rolled up towel inside the garment, directly under the hole, to separate the garment layers and ensure you are attaching the patch to only the area around the hole.

sleeve

towel

3 Tear off a piece of wool roving and ball it up. The ball should be big enough to cover the hole and overlap its perimeter by about ¼ inch. Center the roving over the hole.

roving

Note Your patch doesn't have to be a circle! Place a cookie cutter of any shape directly over the hole and fill it with roving, then hold the cookie cutter in place while needling to create a shaped patch.

4 Place the garment with towel inside on a tabletop or other hard surface. Do *not* needle-felt with your project in your lap! It is very easy to poke through the towel. Hold the barbed needle vertically, and jab it repeatedly into the roving, poking it all over. Be careful of your fingers here. There's no need to push the needle very deep—the towel is there to keep the needle from hitting the table and breaking—but pay special attention to the perimeter of the hole, where the roving overlaps the perimeter. Make sure the needle penetrates through the roving *and* the existing material; this is how the patch will be securely fused onto the garment.

5 Continue poking all over the roving with the needle so the roving fibers intertwine and compact. As you continue, pause occasionally to separate the towel from the sweater to make sure you aren't felting it onto the towel. At first it may seem like the roving isn't attaching to the sweater, but then suddenly—voilà—it does! From time to time, stop and pull up gently on the edges of the roving slightly to confirm this. Inspect the perimeter of the hole to be sure it's covered completely by the roving. Add bits of roving to any area that seems thin or isn't fully overlapping past the edge of the hole. When the roving patch is dense and so integrated with the garment that the patch looks and feels like a seamless part of it, you're finished!

- - - - - - - - - - - - - - - - - -

Note It can be helpful to turn the garment inside out and examine the back side of the hole and roving. This way, you should easily be able to tell whether the hole's perimeter is entirely covered.

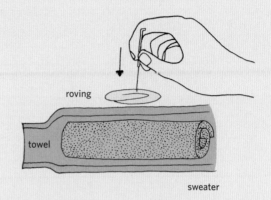

roving

towel

sweater

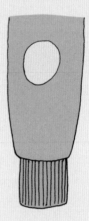

Mending Life

To honor
the gift of your wool
I will mend this hat
over and
over and
over again.

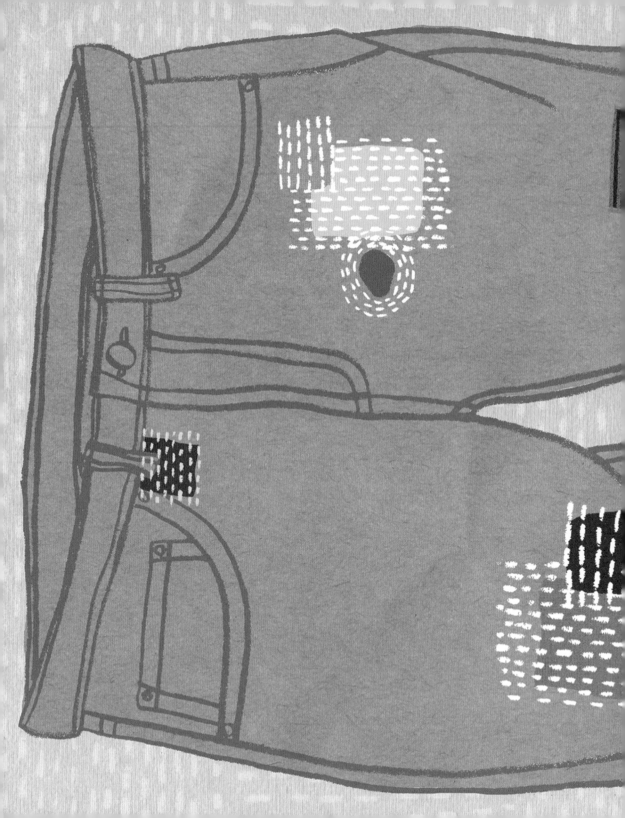

Patching

My friend Madeline is an organic farmer who is hearty, bold, hardworking, visionary, and not the least concerned with wearing the latest fashion. She isn't worried about getting dirty, she chooses not to be dainty or delicate, and she throws herself into any physical task with gusto. When the weather cools, she dons a patched-up down coat, *casually*—the only word that feels right to describe the way she wears everything—as if it doesn't matter one bit. But it does; it matters to her that the coat is still doing what it's supposed to do: keep her warm in the chilly fringes of a long day in the field, no matter the tears in the elbows, flanks, and pockets from snagging on blackberry brambles or errant nails in the toolshed. She needs that coat.

The coat is red. The patches are yellow. I catch glimpses of her out in the field, surrounded by a lush sea of green—kale, chard, peas, bok choy, collards, celery, broccoli. She shimmies backward down the path with a scuffle hoe, her yellow elbows flashing as she weeds. She looks like a colorful sailboat adrift on a vast sea where sky and ocean are the same silver color. She looks like the first spring flower to bloom deep in the forest, the first star to appear in a dusky evening sky, a bold flag proudly announcing what it stands for. She is an Henri Matisse painting, a Romare Bearden collage.

Before I saw Madeline's coat, the thought hadn't even crossed my mind that it was possible to repair a busted down jacket. If it had been my unfortunate luck to spring a leak in my jacket, resulting in a slow bleed of down feathers, I would have lamented the hole, thinking: *These jackets cost an arm and a leg, gah! . . . Why in the world did I lean on that?! . . . So much money down the drain! . . . Such a tiny hole now, but it's going to get so big!*

Then I would have reluctantly handed it off to the thrift store to become someone else's problem, most likely to never keep anyone warm again but be sent straight to the landfill. But when I saw Madeline's mended jacket, I sort of, kind of, just a little bit, wished my own coat had a hole or two, just so I could fix it. When the first hole *does* appear, I'll be ready. I'll mend it with a colorful patch and wear my coat with pride. Undoubtedly, someone else will see my mend, and mend her jacket too.

—Sonya

Mending Life

The Art of Patching

Patches on clothing have seen a wayward journey in meaning. They were essentially a symbol of poverty until the 1960s, when this symbolism was subverted by the hippies and later by the punks who adopted them as an expression of rebellion. Nowadays, sporting a patch suggests that you are mindful of the environment. Patches are even en vogue!

Instead of re-creating fabric to fill a hole as in darning, patching is a technique in which a fabric patch is secured over or under a hole. Patching typically works best on woven fabrics, like denim jeans or cotton button-down shirts, but don't be afraid to try patching on a knit. Elbow patches made from boiled wool, woven fabric, or upcycled leather can look pleasing on a knit sweater.

Choosing the Right Needle

When you're mending something made from delicate fabric, such as a thin cotton blouse, a small needle is appropriate (so as not to poke big holes in the fabric). If you are mending a knit, such as a T-shirt or leggings, you will also want to use a small needle. When mending a heavier fabric, like denim, canvas, or heavyweight cotton, you'll want to use a medium needle. Experiment—if it feels hard to pull the needle and thread through the fabric, switch to a bigger needle; if the needle is making unnecessarily large holes, switch to a smaller needle. If you choose to sashiko over your patch, we recommend using a sashiko needle.

Choosing the Right Thread

The weight of the thread will depend on the fabric being mended. All-purpose thread is thin and fairly durable, perfect for invisible stitches and delicate garments. Button and craft thread is very durable and more visible. The kind of thread you use for sashiko stitching is your choice; sashiko thread and embroidery thread are thick and make for very visible stitches. (See page 32 for our sashiko tutorials.)

Choosing the Right Fabric

Generally it's best to choose a patch fabric that is similar to the fabric of the item you are mending. If your item is woven or made of denim, choose a woven or denim patch. If you're mending a knit, like leggings, choose a knit scrap (perhaps from an old T-shirt or another pair of leggings) to use as a patch. Really light, gauzy material doesn't make a great patch unless it is for a light, gauzy garment. Matching the type of fabric will ensure that the patch has the same qualities as the original and will feel more continuous.

Three Ways to Patch Holes

Here we offer three techniques to patch holes in woven fabric. We've found that the durability of an exterior patch versus an interior patch is the same, so choosing which method to use is mostly an aesthetic choice.

Supplies

- Medium needle

- Button and craft thread or all-purpose thread (in the same color, if desired, as the patch and/or garment)

- Fabric patch at least 1 inch larger on all sides than the hole or tear

- Scissors

- Straight pins

- Iron

- Pinking shears (recommended for cutting out patch fabric so that the edges fray less, particularly for both interior patch techniques)

- Ruler (optional)

- Fabric pencil (optional)

- Embroidery hoop (optional—can be helpful for holding garment and patch taut while sewing)

For the Interior Patch: Exposed Edge Technique (page 101) or if you choose to add sashiko stitching to the Exterior Patch, the following supplies are also necessary:

- Sashiko thread (or embroidery thread)

- Sashiko needle (or embroidery needle)

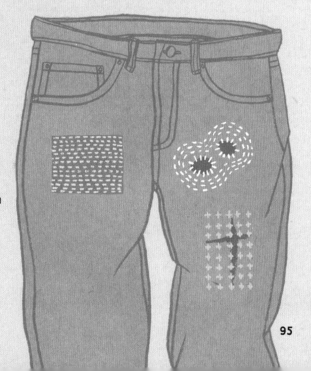

Exterior Patch

This is the most basic and common patching technique. Essentially, you'll be affixing a fabric patch to your garment using the whip stitch. You have the option to add sashiko stitches over the patch for reinforcement and decoration.

1 Clean up the hole by cutting away any ragged edges and loose threads. (If you are mending a tear we recommend sewing big whip stitches to hold the edges of the tear together and stabilize the area before attaching the patch. These stitches will be hidden under the patch.)

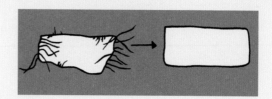

2 If the hole is on a pant leg or a sleeve, roll the leg or sleeve up to make it shorter.

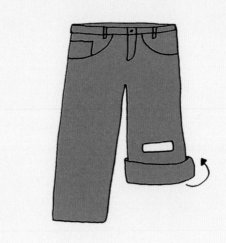

3 Iron the patch fabric flat.

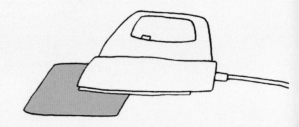

4 Fold the patch edges ½ inch on all sides and press flat with the iron.

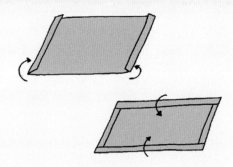

5 Lay the garment flat on a work surface, straightening it out so there are no puckers, ripples, or wrinkles. Carefully slip your hand into the pant leg or sleeve from the bottom and hold it steady as you place the patch, with folded edges face down, over the hole with your other hand.

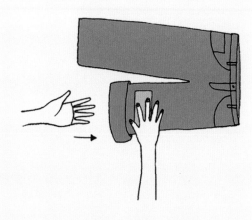

6 Using your hand inside the garment and under the patch, guide the straight pins as you pin the patch to the garment. Be sure to pierce both the patch and the garment with each pin, but be careful not to pin the back of the garment. Pin each corner and add a few pins to each side, about an inch apart. If your patch is very small, you can pin closer together.

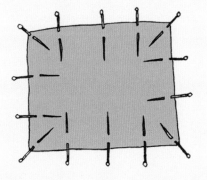

7 Thread a medium needle with a single strand of button and craft thread or a double all-purpose thread and tie a knot. Push the needle under one corner of the patch and pull the thread up through the patch so the knot is hidden between the patch and the garment.

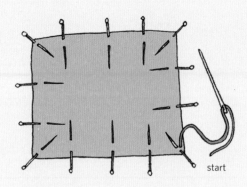

start

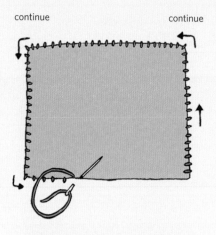

continue   continue

8 Whip stitch (see page 28) the patch to the garment around its perimeter, taking the pins out as you go. The stitches should be small and neat. Stitch in place to finish sewing (see page 26).

9 The patch is now secure. If desired, you can further reinforce the patch by covering it with decorative sashiko stitches (see page 32).

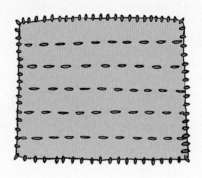

Mending Life

Interior Patch: Tucked Edge Technique

This technique, which looks like reverse appliqué, can be a charming way to mend a hole or cluster of small holes. The tucked edges make for a tidy, attractive mend, while the additional stitching leaves ample room for aesthetic play.

1 Clean up the hole by cutting away any ragged edges and loose threads.

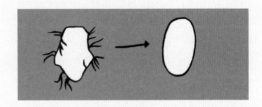

2 Center the patch under the hole on the inside of the garment. (If there is a cluster of holes, you can place one patch under all the holes or a separate patch under each hole.) Pin the patch in place around the edges of the hole, about ½ inch from the hole's edge. (See illustration; the dotted line indicates the patch's position inside the garment.)

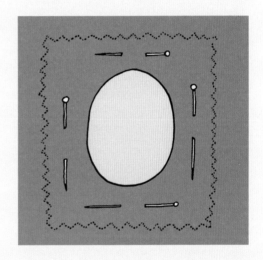

3 Tuck the raw, exposed edges of the hole under, between the garment and the patch, all the way around and pin in place. While this can be challenging, especially if the hole is round, doing your best to tuck under all the edges makes for a tidier mend.

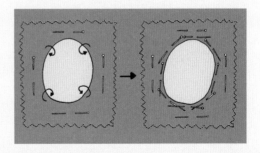

4 Thread a medium needle with a single strand of button and craft thread or a double all-purpose thread and tie a knot. Hide the knot by beginning under the tucked edge of the hole, pushing the needle up through the garment fabric only.

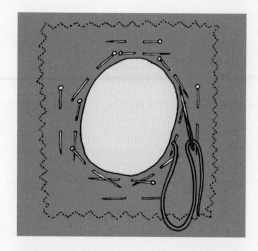

5 Whip stitch (see page 28) around the perimeter of the hole, being sure to sew through both the garment and the patch fabric to secure it. As you stitch, check that the edges stay tucked under. Stitch in place to finish sewing (see page 26).

6 At this point, you have the opportunity to continue with the same thread or change to a contrasting color, or switch to a sashiko needle and sashiko thread for thicker, more visible stitches. Thread your needle and tie a knot. Leaving a distance of about ¼ inch from the hole, sew a running stitch around the circumference through both the patch and the garment fabrics. You can also sew more concentric circles of running stitches or little pluses (see page 36).

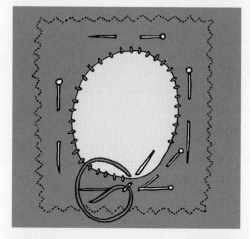

Note We also like to use this technique for mending holes in garments made from knit fabric, like long-sleeve shirts, T-shirts, or leggings. Use knit fabric for the patch. The whip stitch around the hole allows for a surprising bit of stretch, which is optimal as the fabric moves. Keep in mind that the running stitch brings a bit more rigidity to the mend—if you choose to sew concentric running-stitch circles around the mended hole, the fabric in that area will have less stretch.

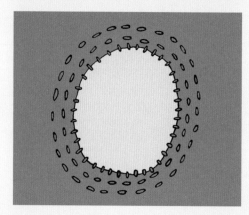

Interior Patch: Exposed Edge Technique

This style of patching doesn't try to hide the ragged, often dramatic damage garments endure. Sashiko stitching is used to attach the patch underneath the tear, leaving the rough edges of the tear exposed. The patch fabric may peek through the tear—an opportunity to choose a fun patch color that contrasts with the garment fabric!

1 Iron the tear and surrounding area so that the fabric is as flat as possible.

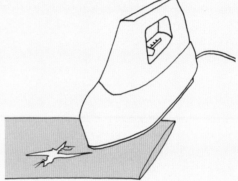

2 Set the garment on a work surface. If working on a pant leg or sleeve, roll up the fabric so that it's easier to insert your hand and reach under the tear. Center the patch under the tear, right side up on the inside of the garment.

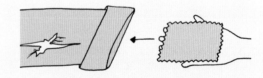

3 Make sure the garment and the patch are lined up and very flat (see illustration; the dotted line indicates the patch's position inside the garment).

4 Secure the patch to the garment by pinning in place. Use your hand inside the garment to guide the pins. Be sure to pin down the edges of the tear also but take care not to pin the other side of the garment.

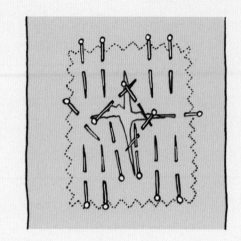

5 Thread a medium needle with a single thread of a contrasting color. No need to knot the end.

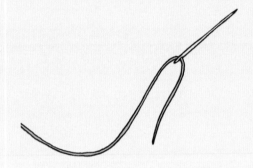

6 Sew basting stitches to hold everything in place, particularly focusing on stitching the edges of the patch and the tear. Basting stitches are essentially very large running stitches. No need to stitch in place at the end, as these basting stitches are temporary. Remove the pins.

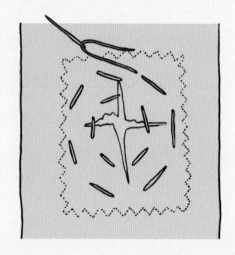

7 You will be attaching the patch to the garment using your choice of sashiko stitching (see page 32). If you'd like to follow a grid for these stitches, use a fabric pencil and ruler to draw one on the exterior of the garment, over the tear and surrounding area. The grid should extend at least 1 inch beyond the tear on all sides. Feel free to skip the grid if you want to sew these reinforcement stitches freehand.

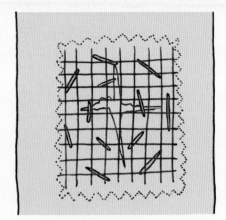

8 Thread a sashiko needle with a single sashiko thread. Sew the horizontal rows of sashiko stitches first. Remove the basting stitches.

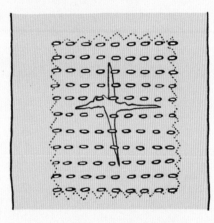

9 Finish the sashiko design as desired. Stitch in place to finish sewing (see page 26).

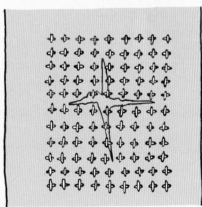

Mending Down Jackets

Colleen Tretter, also known as the Green Darner, is a technical repair seamstress in Bozeman, Montana. Colleen specializes in fixing things people work and play hard in: ski gear, tents, backpacks, sleeping bags, and more. Folks trust Colleen to repair the things that seem totally daunting to tackle on one's own: tears with an explosion of down feathers, slippery nylon fabrics, heavy canvas, busted zippers. But mending unusual materials at home is totally possible. Colleen explains that mostly it boils down to using a very small, sharp needle and not being afraid to mess up. If you are not thrilled with your repair, you can always try again by adding a larger patch over your previous work.

Supplies

- Very small needle (if the one you choose is making alarmingly visible holes as you sew, stop and find a smaller one)

- Nylon or cotton-coated polyester all-purpose thread

- Silk pins

- Woven fabric patch (or even better, nylon material from a stuff sack) that is ¾ inch larger than the hole on all sides

- Ruler

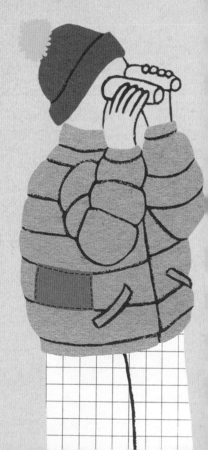

Colleen's advice before beginning: When you first get a tear, until you determine what you'll do to repair it, use Scotch tape or clear packing tape to temporarily close up the hole.

+ +

Note The following instructions are not exclusive to a down jacket. They can also be followed for a vest or sleeping bag of either synthetic or down fill.

Tiny Tear Quick Fix

If the tear in the down jacket is small (½ inch or less), you might be able to sew it closed without a patch. This is not the most elegant method, as it will leave a visible, raised "scar," but it's fast and effective.

1 Thread the needle with a single thread and knot the end. Fold the edges of the tear inward so that the raw edges are tucked in and no longer visible.

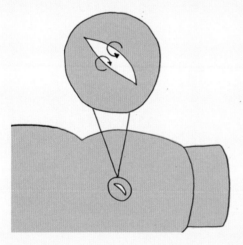

2 Pinch the folded edges together without catching any down. Starting at one end, insert the needle inside the tear and up through one of the sides, then pull the thread taut. This will hide the knot inside the tear.

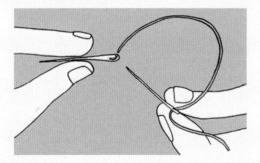

3 Whip stitch (see page 28) the tear closed.

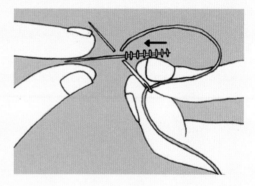

4 Stitch in place to finish sewing (see page 26), then push the needle under the fabric, parallel to the tear, and make it emerge as close as you can to the first stitch on the opposite end of the tear. This buries the thread tail. Cut the thread as close to the fabric as possible.

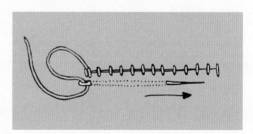

Patching

Larger tears and holes in down jackets will need a patch. As with any patching, it's best to use material that is close in weight and fiber to the garment (in color too, if you like). Most down jackets, whether down or synthetic filled, are ripstop nylon or a similar material. If you can't find a fabric that's a perfect match, don't be deterred. Lots of lightweight woven (but *not* knit) materials will work. Other options are to purchase an embroidered patch or use material from the stuff sack that often accompanies a down jacket or sleeping bag. This technique can be more elegant than the quick fix, especially if you follow the design of the down jacket by making the patch the same size as the divided section in the garment and following along the original seams.

1 To make a patch that matches a divided section, measure the section's height and the patch's desired width and add ¾ inch on all sides. Cut out the patch.

2 Fold the edges of the patch by about ¼ inch. If you are using a synthetic fabric, such as nylon, do *not* iron the folds. Instead, firmly press them repeatedly with your fingernail to make a crease on all sides. If you are using cotton or cotton blend, use an iron to give a quick press to the folds on all sides.

3 Pin the patch carefully in place over the tear/hole using silk pins, hiding the folded edges underneath the patch. You'll want a pin every inch or so around the perimeter of the patch.

4 Thread your needle with a single thread and tie a knot. Push the needle under one corner of the patch and pull the thread up through the patch so the knot is hidden between the patch and the garment. Backstitch (page 30) the patch to the garment around its entire perimeter, stitching directly on top of any existing seams that divide sections. Using a small, even stitch, sew through the outer layer of the jacket only if it is a very thick, puffy down, or through both the outer and inner layers if it is a thinner, base-layer down. Keeping the patch flat can be tricky with such slippery material, but take your time and keep checking as you sew.

5 Stitch in place to finish sewing (see page 26).

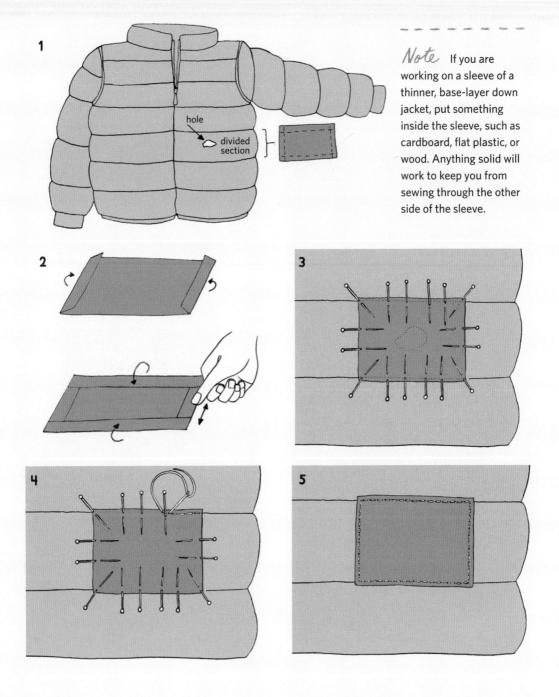

1

hole

divided section

Note If you are working on a sleeve of a thinner, base-layer down jacket, put something inside the sleeve, such as cardboard, flat plastic, or wood. Anything solid will work to keep you from sewing through the other side of the sleeve.

2

3

4

5

Patching Shirt Cuffs

A common sign of a beloved shirt (or jacket) is tattered cuffs. Wear typically occurs along the very edge where the fabric folds at the cuff's end. Adding a patch that fully covers the tattered edge is a simple way to refresh a favorite garment. This technique would work along any garment's edge: pant cuff, waistband, shirt collar, coat bottom hem, or front placket.

Supplies

- Medium needle
- Button and craft thread or all-purpose thread
- Straight pins
- Patch fabric similar in weight to the shirt fabric
- Scissors
- Iron
- Ruler

1 Measure the width of the tattered area. Add 1 inch to determine the width of the patch. To determine the height of the patch, measure how tall the tattered area is, then double the number and add another inch.

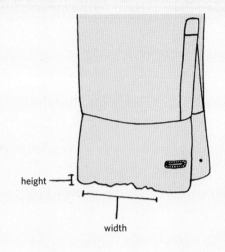

height

width

2 Cut a patch using the dimensions you just determined. Fold each side of the patch ¼ inch and iron the folds flat. Fold the patch in half crosswise with folded edges inside, and iron.

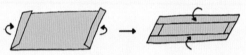

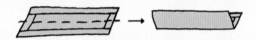

3 (a) Tuck the frayed cuff into the folded crease of the patch, and center the patch over the damaged area.

a

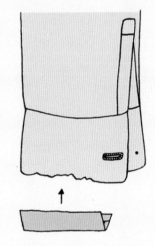

Patching

3 (b) Pin in place. Pins should go through all layers of fabric to hold the patch in place on the outside and inside of the cuff.

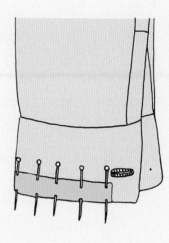

b

4 Thread a needle with a single strand of button and craft thread or a double all-purpose thread. Beginning somewhere along the patch, on the exterior side of the cuff, whip stitch (page 28), picking up only a single layer of the cuff fabric so that the stitches don't go through the inside of the cuff. Leave in pins as you sew so they hold the patch in place inside the cuff.

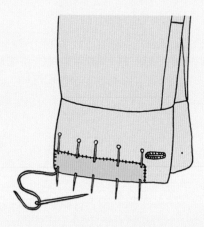

5 Once you are ready to sew the patch on the inside of the cuff, flip the cuff up and keep sewing around the patch perimeter. To finish, stitch in place (see page 26) and remove the pins.

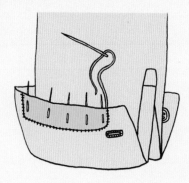

Mending Life

Patching Linens

Bedding tends to wear out in certain spots (usually near a sleeper's feet) because it is often made of thin material, it gets washed frequently, and it may be in use for years. The washing machine is especially rough on bedsheets, often twisting, stretching, and sometimes ripping them if they get caught on the center agitator. But don't fret! You can patch them up quite easily.

1 Follow steps 1 through 7 for an Exterior Patch on pages 96 through 98.

2 Turn the material over to work on the back side of the hole. You want to make the hole tidy by tucking in the raw edges and further secure the material to the patch so a toe or finger won't snag on it. To do this, follow steps 3 through 5 in the instructions for the Interior Patch: Tucked Edge Technique on pages 99 through 100.

Note It's not necessary to tidy up the back side of the hole on a duvet cover, fitted sheet, or pillowcase because the back of the patch isn't exposed and is unlikely to snag.

3 If desired, sashiko stitch over the patch for added strength. If the hole is small, you may not need to do this, but sashiko stitching is recommended for a larger patch (especially if bigger than 4 inches) to help it lie flat and secure against the material.

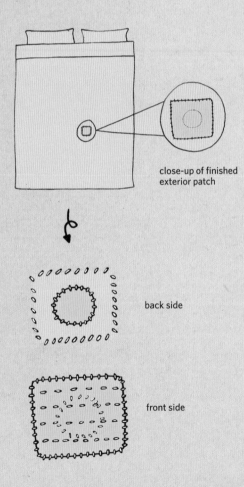

close-up of finished exterior patch

back side

front side

Mending happens all around us.
All the time.

Other Common Repairs

Soon after he moved to Portland, our friend Henry was hired on at a building company. Although he had always been good with his hands, he didn't know a thing about carpentry. At first he found the work intimidating. People entrust a carpenter to work in their house, alongside all their valuable possessions. Anything can go wrong at any time. Henry recounts that early on, he was cutting through a customer's upstairs bathroom floor to replace it when he hit an unexpected buried water pipe—sending water gushing through all three stories of the house (and just barely missing a grand piano). Completely panicked, he couldn't find the shutoff valve in the basement, so he called his boss, Victor, who rushed over. Together they mopped up the house and turned on the air conditioner to dry everything out.

He worried he might lose his job or be reprimanded for the mistake, but not once did Victor express disappointment in Henry. "There's nothing broken that can't be fixed," was Victor's maxim, and he reassured his employees often with this phrase. Victor's confidence in Henry's ability to problem solve, even as a beginner, instilled a stalwart confidence in Henry that persisted as he practiced and practiced and eventually became a master at his craft. Of course, he made many mistakes along the way and still does occasionally, but he has always trusted his ingenuity to figure out how to fix them. When Henry told us Victor's maxim, Nina eagerly scribbled it down on a scrap of paper and stuck it up on our studio wall as words to live by. We've carried this magical phrase with us for years. It reminds us to quell our fears of making mistakes and encourages us to take chances, to be adventurous, and to not get stuck.

If something is broken, what is there to lose in trying to fix it? Why not go forward with gusto? With curiosity? Perhaps many of us fear failure, believing that we will make the problem worse, turning a small hole into an even bigger one. But even if we do, the bigger hole can still be mended. Victor's words remind us not to be so hard on ourselves when we mess up, and they free us from having to worry too much about the outcome of our attempt. When something breaks and we buy a replacement instead of first trying to repair it, we miss out on an important opportunity to hone our problem-solving faculties. And we miss out on an opportunity to feel the deep satisfaction of being the agent of healing.

—Sonya and Nina

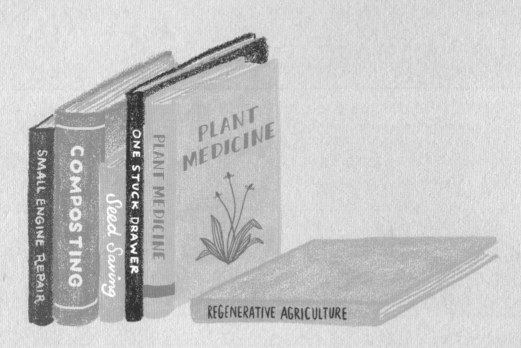

Fixing Snags

Knit and woven fabric both can easily snag, especially if they are of a loose, open knit or weave. At our parents' house, there is a wicker chair with a few broken twigs that always seems like it's reaching out to grab an unlucky sweater that brushes too close by. Many a shirt have snagged there. Though it might be tempting, don't *ever* cut a snag or you'll end up with a big hole! If you get a snag, try this first: smooth and pull the surrounding threads, "massaging" the fabric to hopefully draw the snagged thread back in line without having to take more drastic steps. If that doesn't fix it, follow the steps below.

Supplies

- Small or medium needle

- All-purpose thread (preferably in the same color as the garment)

- Scissors

1 Thread a needle with a single thread 8 to 10 inches long. You don't need to knot the end. Slip the needle through the snag and pull the thread through about 4 inches.

2 Tie the thread to the snag in a double overhand knot (see page 22).

3 Push the needle through the fabric at the base of the snag.

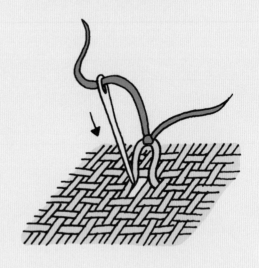

4 Pull the needle all the way through to the underside, pulling the snag through with it.

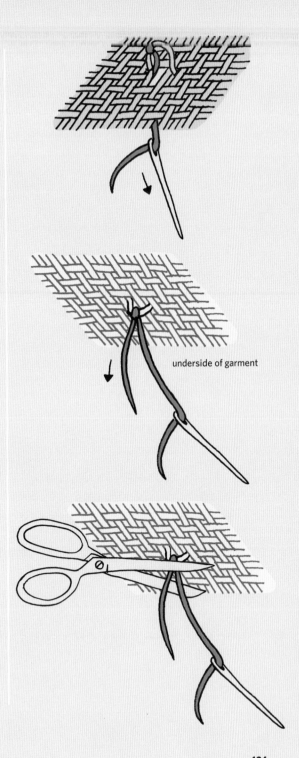

5 Turn the garment inside out and find the needle, thread, and snag. Pull the thread tail through if it is still showing on the outside of the garment (we suggest using the tip of the needle to pick up the tail and pull it through).

underside of garment

6 If you're working on a delicate, lightweight garment, this should be sufficient—cut the thread as close to the knot as possible and you're done. On a bulkier garment with a heavyweight weave, you may want to further secure the snag to the underside. To do this, pick up a couple threads on the underside of the garment, stitch in place twice, and cut the excess thread.

Replacing Buttons

It's good practice to reinforce buttons on clothes when you notice them starting to loosen, well before one goes missing and you need to find a replacement. Stock up on buttons of different colors and sizes so that you have an assortment of pretty ones to choose from if and when you do need one. You can replace a lost button with a close match or choose something completely unique to make a statement. Either way, it's important to select a button of roughly the same diameter of the lost one so that it fits through the corresponding buttonhole.

Supplies

- Button and craft thread or all-purpose thread

- Small needle (for a small button) or medium needle (for a larger one)

- Button

- Fabric pencil

- Straight pin

- Scissors

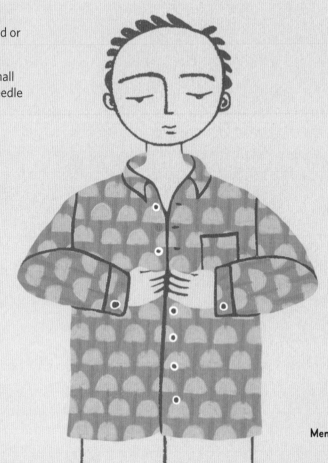

1 Thread a needle with a single strand of button and craft thread or a double all-purpose thread; the resulting length should be about 12 inches. Tie a knot. Position the button on the fabric where the old button used to be. Sometimes thread from the old button remains—this is a good way to know where exactly to sew the new one so that it aligns with the buttonhole. If there are no signs of the original placement, close the garment to see where the buttonhole falls, then use a fabric pencil to mark a dot in the center. Open the garment to double-check that the dot lines up with any other buttons (if there's a row).

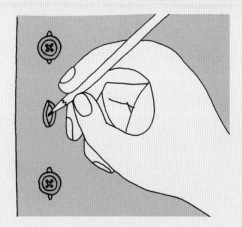

2 We recommend placing a pin underneath the dot that you just drew. This pin will help keep the button slightly elevated off the fabric. Center the new button over the dot.

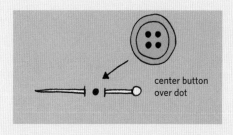

center button over dot

3 Push the needle up through the underside of the fabric and through one hole in the button.

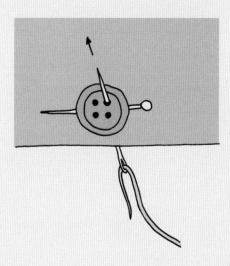

4 Pull on the needle until the knot is snug against the back of the fabric. Turn the needle around and push it back down through the hole diagonal from the one it came up through.

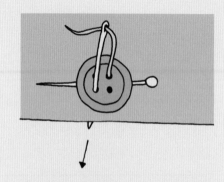

5 Pull the thread taut but not too tight, forming a diagonal stitch across the button.

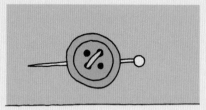

6 Push the needle (a) up through the fabric again and through one of the unused button-holes, and then (b) back down through its diagonal opposite, making an X.

a

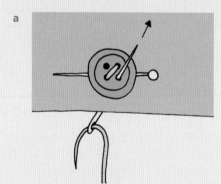

b

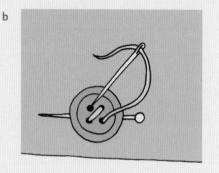

7 Go back over these stitches once or twice more, repeating the X pattern to ensure the button is securely fastened, but be sure not to pull the thread too tightly so there's still some give underneath the button. Remove the pin, if used.

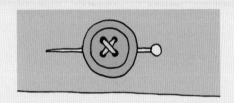

8 Now push the needle up through the fabric only—still under but not *through* the button. Wind the thread around the threads holding the button to the fabric five or six times. This ensures that the button is not sewn too tightly against the fabric, as otherwise it may be hard to put through the buttonhole—a truly frustrating button!

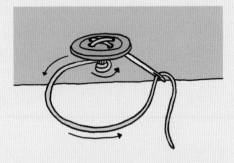

9 Push the needle back down through the fabric and stitch in place to finish sewing (see page 26).

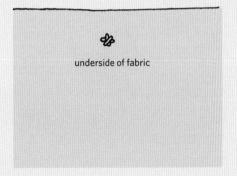

underside of fabric

Reattaching Belt Loops

Belt loops are used for much more than just holding a belt in place—in this era of skinny jeans and low-rise waistlines, they are tugged and yanked and often ripped while hiking up pants. Though machine sewing is the strongest way to reattach a torn belt loop, this is a handy way to mend it without one. Either way, once a belt loop has been repaired, it needs to be handled gently.

Supplies

- Medium needle

- Button and craft thread (in the same color as the pants)

- Ruler

- Patch fabric (preferably denim or another heavyweight woven)

- Straight pins

- Scissors

- Iron (optional)

1 Clean up the loop and hole by cutting away any ragged edges and loose threads. (If your loop has come loose but hasn't torn a hole in your pants, skip to step 6.)

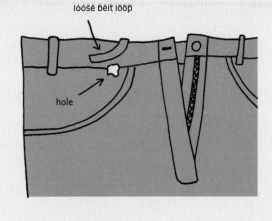

2 If the ripped-off belt loop has left a damaged area in the front of the pants where it used to be attached, you will need to add a patch. To figure out the size of the patch, measure the width and height of the hole, and add ½ inch to all sides. Cut a piece of fabric to these dimensions.

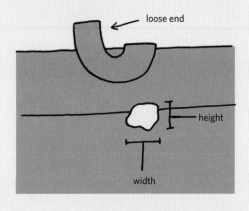

3 Fold all the edges of the patch by ¼ inch, then iron flat.

4 Place the patch, folded edges down, on the outside of the pants, centered and covering the hole. Pin in place.

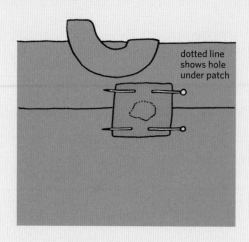

dotted line shows hole under patch

5 Thread a needle with a single strand of button and craft thread and tie a knot. Begin by pushing the needle up through one corner of the patch fabric to hide the knot between the patch and the pants. Whip stitch (see page 28) around the entire perimeter of the patch to secure it to the pants, removing the pins as you go. Stitch in place to finish sewing (see page 26).

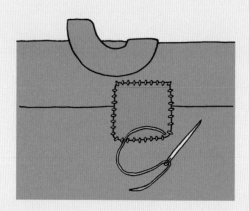

6 Thread the needle again with a single strand of button and craft thread and tie a knot. Place the free end of the belt loop in its original position and pin it in place.

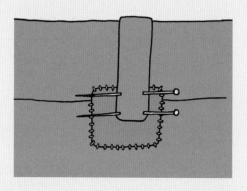

7 Push the needle up through the underside of the belt loop edge and pull the thread taut, hiding the knot between the belt loop and the patch.

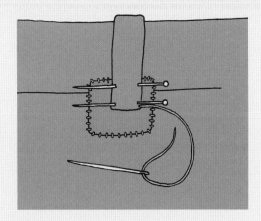

8 Sew the loop to the patch and pants with the backstitch (see page 30), extending beyond the width of the belt loop by a stitch or two in each direction. Be sure to pierce through all three layers of fabric—loop, patch, and pants—with each stitch! Sew back and forth over the loop until it is securely fastened to the patch and pants. Stitch in place to finish sewing (see page 26).

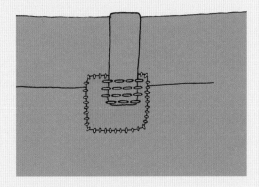

I am learning
to love you again.

Mending Leggings

Inexpensive, versatile, and particularly susceptible to snags, tears, and runs, knit leggings are a prime example of a garment that's often regarded as disposable. When a run appears, it may seem easiest just to buy a new pair, but satisfaction can be found by mending the thin, stretchy material.

The technique to use will depend on the size of the damage. If you are able to catch a hole early, when it is still very small (say, the size of a pencil eraser), three or four quick whip stitches to close the hole or run will often suffice. If the hole is bigger than a pencil eraser, you'll want to follow the instructions for the Interior Patch: Tucked Edge Technique (page 99) or the Interior Patch: Exposed Edge Technique (page 101), being sure to use a patch material similar to your legging fabric. If you have a more extensive run or tear, we recommend sewing it up with a whip stitch as outlined here. These techniques are also applicable to other knit garments, like long-sleeve shirts, and are especially successful on black or pattern-printed fabrics because the mend will be less obvious.

Supplies

- Small needle

- Button and craft thread or all-purpose thread (in the same color as the leggings)

- Scissors

1 Thread a needle with a single strand of button and craft thread or a double all-purpose thread, but don't knot the end. Insert your non-sewing hand inside the leggings to prevent accidentally sewing the leg closed. Attach the thread to the leggings by sewing three stitches in place at one end of the run (or to one side of the hole). You do *not* want to use a knot for this mend because leggings are so thin you may see the knot or feel it against your skin.

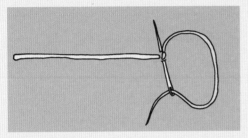

2 Start by pinching together the end of the run where your thread is attached while tucking under any raw edges. Whip stitch (see page 28) across the run or hole by inserting the needle very close to the edge of the run or hole and grabbing the least amount of fabric possible. The closer the stitches are to the edge and the tinier your stitches are, the less puckering there will be in this mended spot. Continue to tuck in any raw edges and pull the thread taut as you sew, cinching the stitches and the run closed.

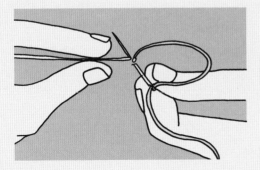

3 When you reach the end of the run, pull the thread tight to cinch the hole closed. Stitch in place to finish sewing (see page 26).

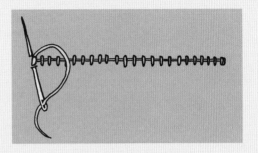

Reinforcing the Seat in Pants

There are few places so constantly subjected to wear as the pant seat, and the spot where inner thighs rub together. These areas are especially problematic for bike commuters, whose inner thighs rub against the bicycle seat. In addition to inevitably breaking down, most jeans are now made with a blend of cotton and synthetics—such as elastane—for stretch, which quickly becomes distended and shapeless with wear. With this tutorial, you can reinforce an area that has begun to wear out by adding a patch to the inside of the garment and stitching it in place using your choice of sashiko stitches (see page 32).

Pay close attention to these susceptible areas for lightening in color, fraying, thinning, and the fabric beginning to lose its shape—any of these indicate it's a good time to add a patch inside for reinforcement. Catching wear in the crotch and inner thigh area early allows for a more discreet repair before it turns into an obvious and much more complicated mending project (see note on page 136).

Supplies

- Medium needle

- Sashiko or embroidery needle

- All-purpose thread (in a contrasting color)

- Sashiko or embroidery thread (in the same color as the pants)

- Straight pins

- Scissors

- Woven fabric piece that is ½ to 1 inch larger on all sides than the worn spot

- Ruler

- Fabric pencil

- Pinking shears (optional)

WORK WEAR

A lot of work wear is made from heavy-duty fabric, such as denim and canvas. If you have access to a sewing machine and know how to use it, mending with a machine is the strongest way to repair work wear—but it can also be frustrating trying to sew through multiple layers of heavy fabric and over bulky seams. In these cases, hand-sewing is the way to go! Here are a few tips:

- Use a heavy-duty thread, like button and craft, and a larger needle suited to make bigger holes for the heavier thread to slide through.

- If you find yourself struggling to pull the needle and thread through the fabric, especially on seams or other areas with multiple layers of fabric, needle-nose pliers can be helpful to better grip the needle and pull it through the fabric.

- Coating the thread with wax is also an option for adding strength and glide: pull the thread across a bar of beeswax before sewing.

- Cut out a patch that is quite a bit larger than the problem area (at least 1 inch on each side, but there's nothing wrong with going larger!) just to be sure that you are sewing it onto very stable fabric.

- When sewing, use the backstitch for added strength.

1 Decide which sashiko design you will use for reinforcement (see page 32). Keep in mind that depending on where the threadbare area is and the color of thread you choose, these stitches may be visible. If you'd like to follow a grid, use a fabric pencil and ruler to draw it on the outside of the pants, covering an area that is at least 1 inch larger on all sides than the threadbare spot.

2 (a) Lay the pants on a work surface. Center the patch fabric inside the pants under the threadbare area. (See illustration; the color blue indicates the fabric on the inside of the pants, *under* the threadbare area.) (b) Hold it flat and in place with one hand inside the pants while pinning the fabric from the outside. Take care while pinning to keep everything flat.

3 Thread the needle with a single all-purpose thread. Sew a basting stitch around the perimeter of the patch to hold everything in place. Basting stitches are essentially very large running stitches. No need to stitch in place at the end, as these basting stitches are temporary. Remove the pins.

4 Follow the instructions for the sashiko design you've chosen, then secure the reinforcement patch in place under the threadbare area. Once the stitches are complete, remove the basting stitches. With pinking shears (if using), trim away any extra reinforcement fabric inside the pants that isn't sewn down.

+ +

Note If you have a hole to mend in the crotch or seat of your pants, follow these same mending instructions; just be sure to carefully pin and baste the edges of the hole before sewing any sashiko stitches so the pants fabric is secured. You can also follow either of the interior patching techniques (see pages 99 through 103). It is crucial when mending this area to keep the original shape of the pants. If you have access to a sewing machine, you can machine stitch back and forth over the patch and surrounding area with dense, overlapping lines of stitches to create a really fortified mend.

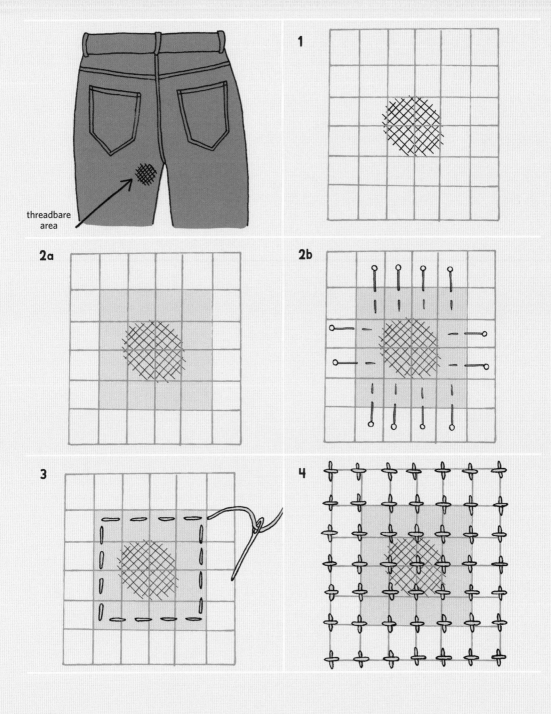

threadbare
area

1

2a

2b

3

4

Mending Underarm Holes

The seams under the arms of a shirt are under constant strain and friction. Quite often the fabric in this area wears thin or the seams come apart. This can be a tricky place to mend since it is at the junction of four seams. It may be difficult to achieve an invisible mend in this area because when a hole goes unnoticed or unattended for very long, the fabric can become warped, making it harder to match the seams. As always, it's best to take action when you first discover a problem. Here, we imagine you've caught the hole in time: it is small and along a seam. You'll essentially be restitching the missing seam with a sturdy backstitch.

Supplies

- Small needle (for a delicate fabric) or medium needle (for medium to heavy fabric)

- Button and craft or all-purpose thread (preferably in the same color as the shirt)

- Straight pins

- Scissors

1 Turn the shirt inside out.

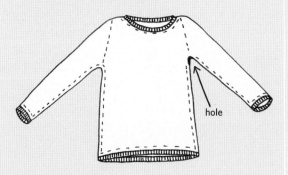

hole

2 Match up the sides of the hole so that the seams lie flat. Pin the sides together.

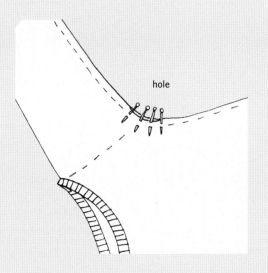

hole

3 Thread the needle with a single strand of button and craft thread or a double all-purpose thread and tie a knot. Beginning on top of the intact seam about an inch before the hole, backstitch along the seam (see page 30), removing the pins as you go.

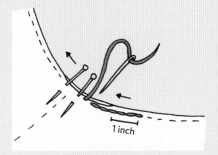

1 inch

4 Continue sewing beyond the hole by about an inch, again overlapping the intact seam. Stitch in place to finish sewing (see page 26).

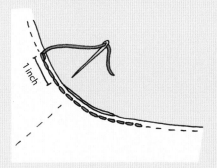

1 inch

+ +

Note If the hole is large or the fabric is distended around it, it may be worth adding an exterior or interior patch made from similar fabric (such as jersey material from a T-shirt). See the instructions for an Exterior Patch on page 96 or the tutorial for the Interior Patch: Tucked Edge Technique on page 99.

Two Ways to Mend Pants Pockets

A hole in a pocket is so frustrating. Spare change, keys, hairpins, or other small objects are set free and you might not realize it until they're gone. Here we explain two simple ways to mend a hole in a front pant pocket. The first resolves a hole where the seam along the edge of the pocket bag has come undone using a simple backstitch. The second way addresses a small hole in the side of the pocket bag fabric by adding a patch.

Supplies

- Medium needle
- Button and craft thread
- Straight pins
- Scissors

- Patch fabric (if patching the hole)
- Iron (optional)

Restitching the Seam

1 Turn the pants inside out. Inspect the pocket bag to identify where the seam has come apart, and cut away any loose threads.

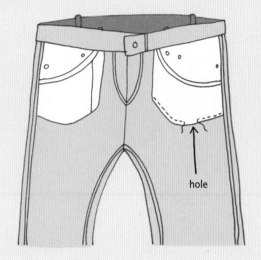

hole

2 Flatten out the pocket bag, ironing if needed, and realign the seams.

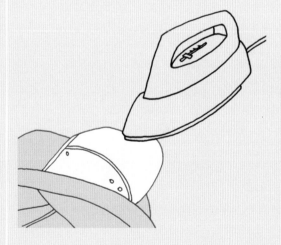

3 Thread the needle with a single strand of button and craft thread and tie a knot. Beginning about an inch before the start of where the seam has come undone, sew small backstitches (see page 30) along the original seam. Continue sewing along where the old seam was and past by about an inch to overlap the intact seam.

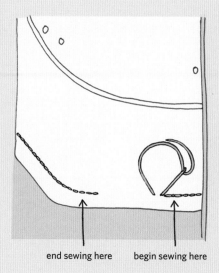

end sewing here   begin sewing here

4 Stitch in place to finish sewing (see page 26).

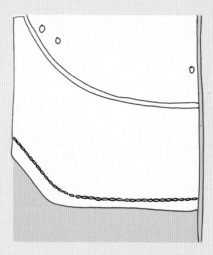

Patching Holes

1 With your pants right side out, pull the pocket bag inside out. You'll be patching on the inside of the pocket bag, which is now on the outside.

2 Follow steps 1 through 7 in the Exterior Patch tutorial on pages 96 through 98. When pinning, make absolutely sure you are only pinning the patch to the fabric around the hole and not to the other side of the pocket bag—otherwise, you will be sewing the pocket closed! You can put your hand inside the pocket bag while you work to ensure this doesn't happen.

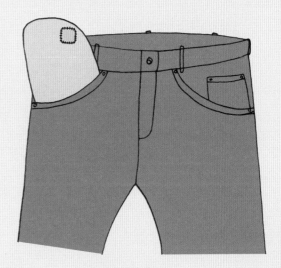

We need more fix-it shops!
Owned by moms & pops.

Places of resurrection,

Second lives, second chances,
thirds, fourths, fifths...

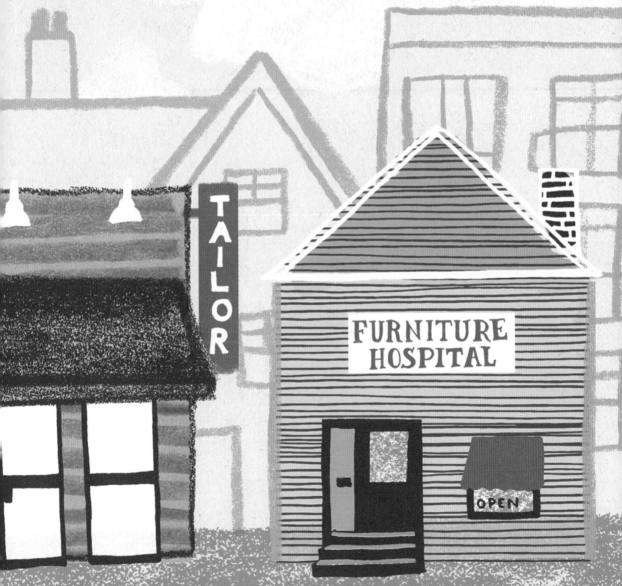

Zipper Repair

Zippers are everywhere: on jeans, boots, purses, luggage, sleeping bags, and tents; and yet, they're completely mystifying to most of us. When they break it often means the end of the line for the item, but it doesn't have to be! We consulted our local cobbler, Julie Derrick of JD's Shoe Repair, for simple instructions on how to fix a stuck zipper slider on a nylon coil zipper. You can identify a nylon coil zipper by looking closely at the zipper teeth—they form a continuous coil chain and this coil is stitched onto the zipper fabric. The zipper slider often gets stuck at an area under constant strain (like the ankle of a boot) when the stitches holding the zipper coil to the fabric break and the teeth become misaligned. In this tutorial, Julie shares how to sew the coil back onto the fabric so the slider can move the teeth into correct position and zip together. (Please note that if you have problems with a metal or plastic zipper, we advise taking it to your local cobbler.)

Supplies

- Small needle

- Nylon thread (preferable) but cotton-coated polyester all-purpose thread will do

- Small snips or scissors

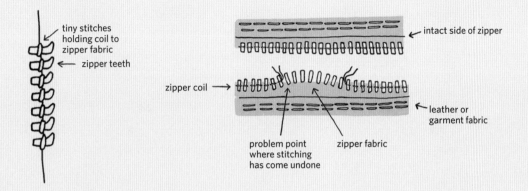

tiny stitches holding coil to zipper fabric

zipper teeth

zipper coil →

← intact side of zipper

← leather or garment fabric

problem point where stitching has come undone

zipper fabric

1 Thread the needle with a double thread and tie a knot. If you can pull or push the teeth back into alignment, do so first. It helps to use the blunt end of a needle to maneuver the tiny teeth. Flatten them out as much as you can. Even if the coil is splayed, you can usually get them back into a pretty uniform position. If you can't, the zipper may be too far gone for this repair (but a professional may still be able to fix it). Snip any loose threads from the zipper fabric.

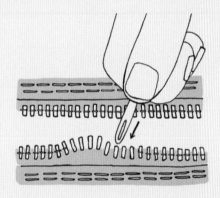

2 Begin by sewing a running stitch (see page 27) over a few of the existing intact stitches just before the problem area.

Note Try to match the manufacturer's stitches that are still intact. The slider will be less likely to catch on your stitches if they align with the original in size and position.

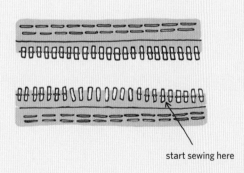

start sewing here

3 As you reach the misaligned teeth, keep sewing running stitches so that the needle and thread weave over and under the teeth: pull the needle up between two teeth and pull the thread tight, then push the needle down between the next two teeth, through the zipper fabric.

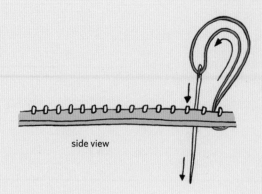

side view

4 Weave over a tooth, down through the zipper fabric, and come up just beyond the next tooth. Continue in this manner. Sew beyond the problem area with a few stitches over the original intact stitches.

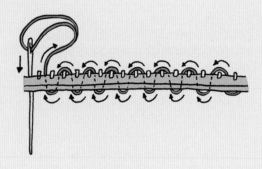

5 Turn around and sew running stitches in the opposite direction, reversing the stitch pattern; if you stitched under a tooth before, now stitch over that tooth, and vice versa.

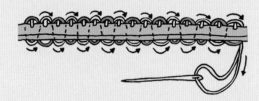

6 When you reach the first stitch you made, finish sewing by pushing your needle through to the underside of the work. (a) Thread the needle through the last stitch. (b) Before pulling it tight, pass the needle through the loop in the thread, making a knot. Pull the thread taut. Repeat this two more times to secure the stitching, then cut the thread. From here on, this zipper is on light duty. Be gentle when zipping, especially over this spot. The same spot can be stitched like this repeatedly, so check it regularly.

a
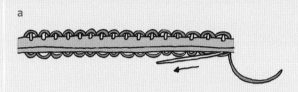

b
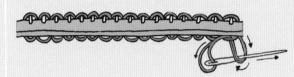

SUPPORT THE REPAIR ECONOMY

If a problem with a garment seems beyond your capacity to fix, it is a great idea to have your local tailor or cobbler take a look. We need to support the repair economy by keeping these professionals in business! "It's a real honor to be able to take care of shoes," Julie, our cobbler, tells us. "They are the one item in your wardrobe that literally goes everywhere with you. They know all. They quietly absorb the sweat and mediate between your feet and the sidewalk, bearing all the weight and pressure of every footfall. For me, to care for and mend this part of a person's life is humble and rewarding work; it just makes sense." Not everyone can make time to mend or has the desire to learn more advanced skills, and not everyone has to. It is equally good to ask someone else to do the mending, particularly with more complex repairs.

Beyond a Mend

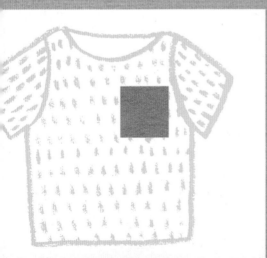

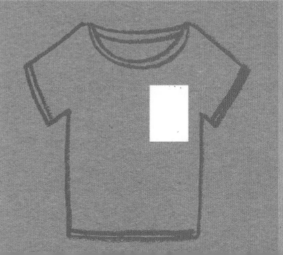

When I was a child, I naturally sensed that objects around me had a living quality. I thought that I might hurt a toy's feelings if I gave it away or if I chose to play with another toy. Even our small urban backyard felt animate; the grass buzzed with insects and fairies, and I had the sense that a large stone along the path to our entryway greeted me every time I got home from school.

Even as an adult, I've caught glimpses of the same animate world: on a walk in the woods a particular gnarled tree will snag my attention as most certainly being alive with personality, and I've always had the suspicion that just as I love wearing my favorite shoes, they love fulfilling their purpose of walking me through the world.

I like the idea of a thing having a soul—I might then hold it in my hand more gently or whisper an acknowledgment of its service to me. Cultures all over the world throughout the centuries have believed in animism, or the living quality of everyday objects, and have lived in a way that honors them.

A particularly beautiful example of this is a four-hundred-year-old Buddhist and Shinto festival in Japan called Hari-Kuyō, or the Festival of Broken Needles. This day is marked by a memorial to the sewing needles and pins that served those who used them throughout the year.

To give thanks to the things that work hard for us recognizes the gift in all that surrounds us and supports our well-being. We come to see that we are woven into a great web of relationships in a very alive world.

—Nina

Hemming Pants

When we were in high school in the early 2000s, we desperately wanted our pants to completely cover our shoes (it was the only cool way back then), so we schemed how to add fabric at the bottom hems to make them longer and "flared." Now that we're older, we find ourselves doing just the opposite, hemming pants to make the perfect high-waters. Here's a quick way to make any pants fall just right. You can also use this tutorial to adjust the hem at the bottom of a dress or skirt.

Supplies

- Small needle
- Button and craft thread (in the same color as the pants)
- Straight pins
- Seam ripper
- Scissors
- Pinking shears
- Fabric pencil
- Ruler
- Iron

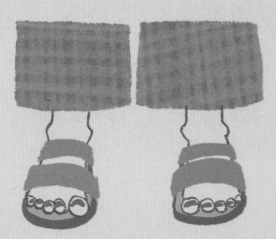

1 Turn the pants inside out. If they already have a hem, pick out the existing stitches using a seam ripper.

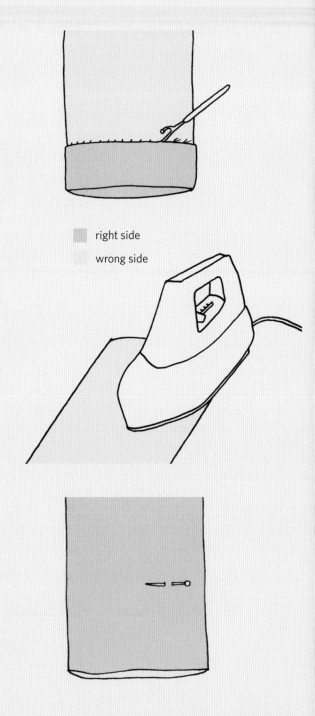

right side

wrong side

2 Flatten out the hem and iron the bottom of the pant legs to smooth any creases.

3 Turn the pants right side out and try them on. Put on the shoes you're most likely to wear with them to be sure of the desired length. Ask a friend to place a pin on the pant leg to indicate this new desired length. If you're alone, you can figure out the placement of the pin by matching the pants up to another pair of pants you have that fit well and placing the pin where the bottom of the well-fitted leg falls.

4 Remove the pants. Measure from the pin to the bottom of the pant leg. If the length is more than 1 inch, consider cutting off the excess so that the length below the pin is not more than 1 inch. Use pinking shears when cutting to reduce fraying.

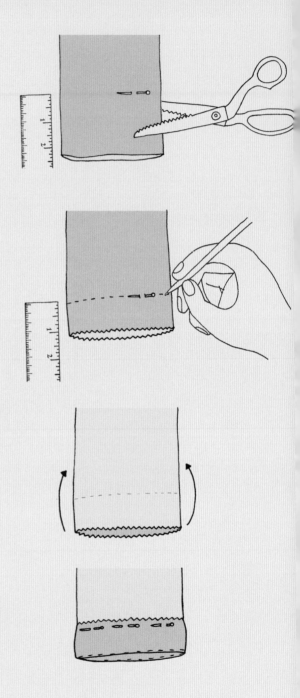

5 Lay the pants flat on a work surface. Using a fabric pencil, mark a dashed line at the height of the pin the whole way around. This will help keep your hem straight.

6 Take out the pin and turn the pants inside out again. Fold up the pant leg, matching the fold to the dashed line you marked. Pin all around to secure the hem.

Mending Life

7 Iron the fold of the pant legs. Try on the pants again to be sure they are the desired length. Make adjustments as needed.

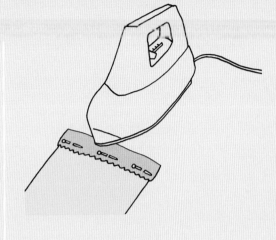

8 There are many good ways to sew up a hem by hand, but we prefer the blind hem stitch. The goal is a stitch that is nearly invisible on the outside of the pants. To do this, thread a needle with a single strand of button and craft thread and tie a knot. Be sure that your pants are inside out again. Insert the needle under the edge of the folded fabric, hiding the knot between the two layers of fabric.

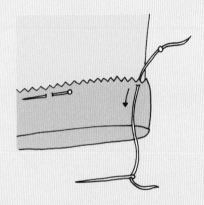

9 The sewing direction is from right to left. Pick up onto the needle just a few threads of the pant fabric above and to the left of where it was pulled through the folded fabric, so that you are making a diagonal stitch. Pull the thread taut.

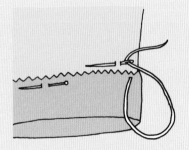

10 Using the needle, again pick up just a few threads of *only* the folded fabric below and to the left of where the thread just came through above. Be sure your needle is going through only one layer of the fabric that is folded up; this tiny stitch will be invisible on the right side of the pants. Pull the thread taut. Remove the pins as you go.

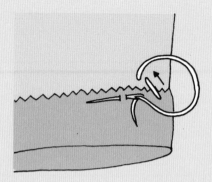

11 Again, pick up just a few threads of the fabric on the needle above and to the left of where it was pushed through the folded fabric below. Pull the thread taut.

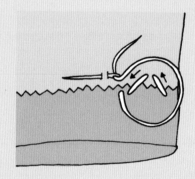

12 And again, pick up just a few threads of the folded fabric on the needle below and to the left of where the thread just came through the fabric above. Pull the thread taut.

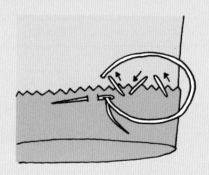

13 Repeat this stitching around the entire hem until you reach where you began. So that the end of your stitching is not visible on the right side of the pants, stitch in place to finish sewing (see page 26) but only sew through the folded-up fabric of the hem.

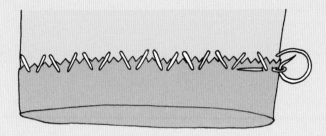

14 Turn the pants right side out. You should only barely see one row of tiny stitches!

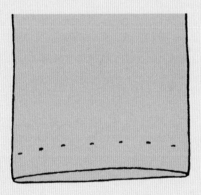

Taking in Garments

Too big, too wide, too baggy. You can easily take in the side seams of a shirt, skirt, or pant leg by using basic sewing skills and a trial-and-error approach. It is wise to practice taking in a seam on a T-shirt or pajama pants you don't care about first so that you get the hang of the technique before working on a favorite garment.

Supplies

- Small or medium needle
- Button and craft thread (in two colors: one similar to the garment color, the other in a contrasting color)
- Straight pins

- Fabric pencil
- Scissors
- Pinking shears
- Iron

1 Try on the garment inside out and locate the area that feels too baggy. Pinch the excess fabric to get a feel for what will feel like a better fit—this excess is what you're going to get rid of. Make a small mark with a fabric pencil across the existing seam at the "top" and the "bottom" of the baggy area. In our example, the shirt fits well in the armpit and waist but feels baggy at the chest and midsection. The fix will be to resew the seam between the armpit and waist to get a better fit.

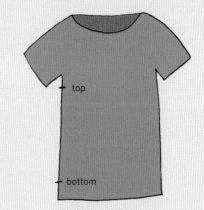

2 Take the garment off and iron it flat (still inside out).

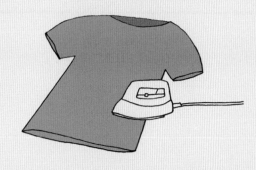

3 Using a fabric pencil, draw a curved line between the two marks you've made (see illustration for details). The line should start at the top mark ("top") and gradually stray away from the existing seam toward the center of the garment ("middle"), then gradually creep back to the existing seam near the bottom mark ("bottom"). It is best to be conservative at first with the distance between the old seam and the new sewing line.

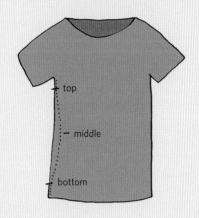

4 Pin along the drawn line, holding the two layers of fabric aligned and flat for sewing.

5 Draw the top and bottom marks on the seam on the opposite side of the garment and draw a curved line between these two marks, basically a mirror of the first line. Pin along this line too.

6 Thread a needle with a single thread in a contrasting color (for easy removal later). No need to tie a knot. Using extralarge running stitches, baste on top of the existing seam 1 to 2 inches above the top mark you made ("top"). Sew on top of the line you marked out with the fabric pencil until you reach the bottom mark ("bottom"). Keep sewing past this mark, rejoining the existing seam and sewing on top of it, for 1 to 2 inches. Baste the opposite seam the same way.

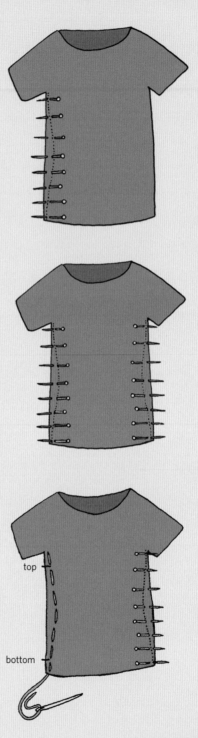

7 Turn the garment right side out and try it on. If it still feels too baggy or ill-fitting, you can go back and sew another line of basting stitches inside the ones you just sewed, adjusting as needed.

8 Turn the garment inside out and thread your needle with a single thread in a similar color to the garment color and tie a knot. Using small backstitches, sew on top of the correct basted seams on both sides of the garment. Stitch in place to finish sewing (see page 26). Remove basting stitches.

9 Depending on how much fabric is now inside the garment with the new seams, you may want to cut the excess material away with pinking shears if it seems bulky inside the shirt. However, if there isn't an annoying amount of excess fabric, don't cut anything. It's a good general rule to avoid cutting if you can, because cut edges will eventually fray and can weaken a garment.

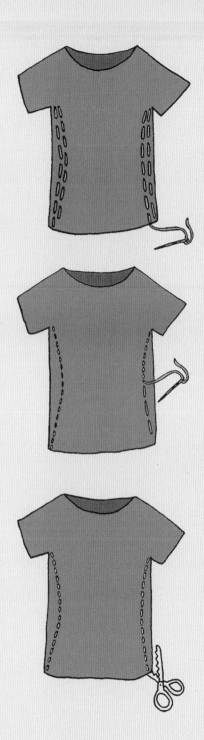

I won't give up on you.
You have so much more to give.

Yes, things do eventually reach a point where they are beyond repair. But here are a few ideas for what to do with your clothes (or bedsheets, tablecloths, curtains, etc.) once they are beyond repair, so they still have a life.

camera strap

handkerchief

stuffed toy

braided rugs, rag rugs

bloomers
cloth bib

cleaning rags

dish towels

cloth pouch

quilt

reusable produce bag

add a pocket

Adding Basic Pockets

Adding a pocket can be a brilliant way to refresh the look of a garment, cover a stain, or add functionality. Use a contrasting fabric to spice up a garment and make it unique. For the purpose of this tutorial, we will explain the steps for adding a breast pocket to a shirt, but the same instructions can be followed for adding one to a jacket, skirt, dress, or apron.

Supplies

- Small needle

- Button and craft thread or all-purpose thread

- Pocket fabric (we recommend a knit fabric, such as jersey, for T-shirts and a woven fabric for woven garments)

- Straight pins

- Pencil

- Fabric pencil

- Scissors

- Ruler

- Iron

- Sheet of scrap paper

1 Try on the garment you plan to add a pocket to. Use a ruler to estimate the size of the pocket you'd like to add, then remove the garment. In our example, we have chosen a 4-by-4-inch pocket. Add 1 inch at the top of the pocket and ½ inch on each of the other three sides for seam allowance. Ours would result in a 5-by-5½-inch rectangle.

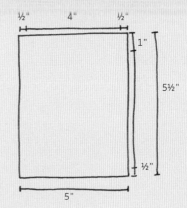

2 On a sheet of scrap paper, measure and mark the rectangle, then cut it out. This is the pattern for your pocket.

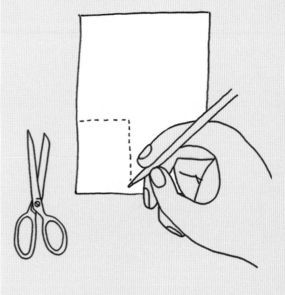

3 Fold in the two sides and the bottom of the paper pattern by ½ inch; fold the top of the rectangle by 1 inch.

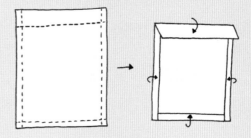

4 Position the paper pattern on the garment where the pocket will go. Pin the sides and bottom of the pattern to the garment, then try it on again to ensure you like the pocket placement.

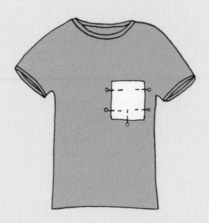

5 When the pocket is in the right spot, remove the garment and lay it flat on a work surface. Using a fabric pencil, mark dots on the garment at each of the four corners of the pattern.

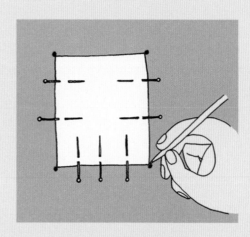

6 Remove the pins from the paper pattern and unfold the edges. Place the pattern on your chosen pocket fabric and pin in place.

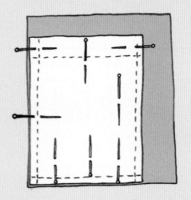

Mending Life

7 Use scissors to cut around the paper pattern.

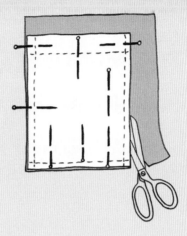

8 Fold over the sides and bottom of the pocket fabric by ½ inch and press with an iron.

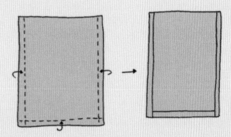

9 Now fold the top edge down by ½ inch and then by ½ inch again. This makes up the pocket's top hem. Press with an iron and pin in place.

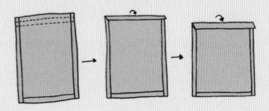

10 Thread a needle with a double all-purpose thread or a single strand of button and craft thread and tie a knot. About ⅜ inch from the top edge of the pocket, sew a small backstitch (see page 30) along the pocket hem, taking out the pins as you go. Finish sewing by stitching in place (see page 26).

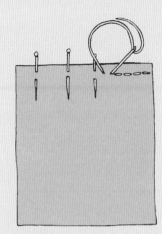

11 Match the pocket with the dots you marked on the garment to position it in place, pinning along the sides and bottom. Sew a small whip stitch (see page 28) along the three sides to attach the pocket to the garment. Stitch in place to finish sewing (see page 26).

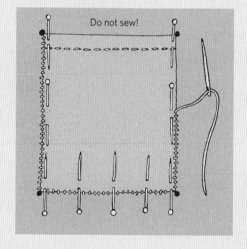

Note It may seem obvious, but it's an easy mistake to make—do not sew the top of the pocket to the garment! This is the pocket opening.

An Open Letter to the Woman Who Made My Shirt

My stitches pitter-patter over yours, the needle whirring up and down in a blur along a frayed seam. My stitches echo, layer, reinforce, empathize, and join with yours, in a dance of over-under, over-under. I am sitting in front of my sewing machine, guiding the fabric through, just as you did when you imprinted this garment with its first row of stitches. This garment was likely one of dozens of the same garment you made that day, not singular in the way I perceive it in my closet. Yet this particular garment is our dialogue, a conversation between us that spans time and space, a momentary overlap of the destinies of two humans who will never meet. In my mind I see your beautiful hair, braided down your back, but your face is hidden from me; I cannot make it out. I watch you sew quickly, with urgency and concentration, but also with boredom, with monotony. I wonder about your morning, your evening, your family, the moments when you relax, your dreams, what you think is beautiful. I wonder how you perceive life. I wonder how you perceive me.

I vow to honor your work by reviving this garment, time and time again, to make it last by reinforcing its seams, patching holes, reweaving threads. These stitches are a tiny offering, my gratitude to you.

—Nina

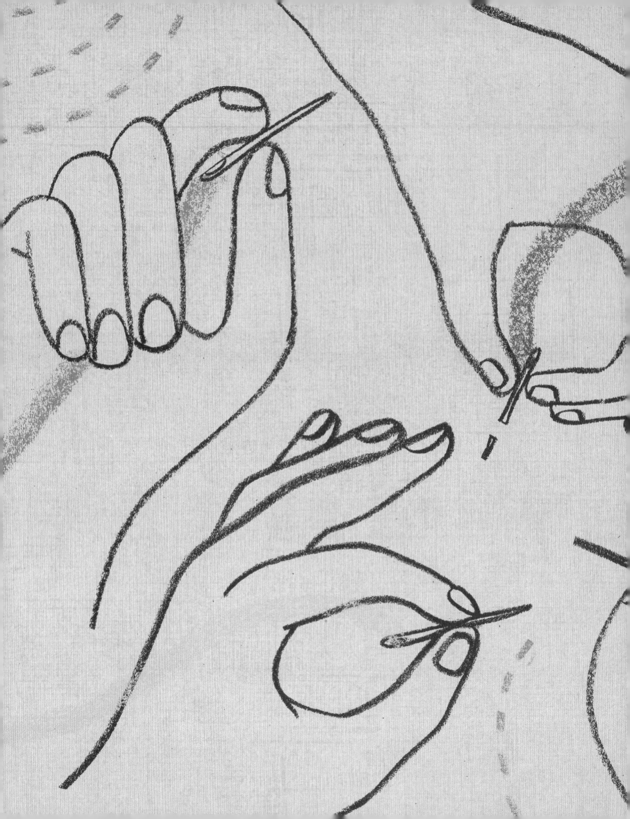

We exist in the in-between.
We are surrounded by things,
yet we hardly know their origin
and we rarely see their final fate.

We mend to remember
where we came from
and
where we need to go.

Lucid and awake
to the before and after,
we burst forth with creativity,
boldness,
needle, and thread.

Mend for a Friend

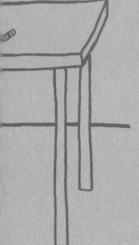

A few years ago, a French sculptor arrived at our doorstep, offering to fix anything we needed on our farm in exchange for room and board. He was traveling across the country this way, never paying a dime for food or a warm bed. He repaired our battered gates, sticky latches, and broken gardening tool handles, and we housed him, fed him, and mended his clothes. It was a beautiful example of the barter economy in action, where we rely less on corporations outside of our community to meet our needs and more on each other, building resilience. Mending bucks the status quo in this way—it means less shopping and more sharing! Once every couple of months we gather with friends for a "mending circle." Sometimes we make it a potluck and share a meal beforehand. Fixing your clothes can feel like way less of a chore when you make it social by mending alongside friends. Now that you too know how to mend, dear reader, you have a skill of great value to offer. Mend for a friend or teach someone else how.

Final Thoughts

One evening we rushed out the door to take a walk in the fading light. Nina threw on her roommate's overalls and Sonya put on a jacket she bought at a childhood friend's moving sale. While walking along the trail, we talked about how Nina was wearing a thin golden ring that was her mother-in-law's and boots our mom owned when she was in college, while Sonya was wearing a hand-me-down shirt she got from her dear friend at a clothing swap and a sweatshirt from a past beau. Nearly every garment on our bodies once belonged to people we love, and we suddenly felt the profundity of this realization. We were being embraced by our dearest family and friends through their clothing.

Our clothes take care of us. They are our protective shell, our second skin, our closest embrace. They encircle us gently and keep us dry, warm, and cozy. Because of this job well done, even the cheapest of clothes are deserving of our care and attention when they break.

There's nothing broken that can't be fixed. That old saying comes to mind again. What if we could really believe it and apply it to everything in our lives? Just as we choose not to give up on an old busted pair of jeans, we choose to heal a friendship, we choose to let go of an old grudge we've been carrying around, and we choose to acknowledge feelings that have been hurt. The most vulnerable members of our society—the houseless, mentally ill, incarcerated—are cast out and disposed of. Can we learn to say, "I won't give up on you" and truly practice it?

When we mend, we are participating in the healing of the world, as mending is a profound act of restoring integrity to an object and our relationship to it. "We need acts of restoration, not only for polluted waters and degraded lands, but also for our relationship to the world," indigenous botanist Robin Wall Kimmerer said. "We need to restore honor to the way we live, so that when we walk through the world we don't have to avert our eyes with shame, so that we can hold our heads up high and receive the respectful acknowledgment of the rest of the earth's beings."[3]

We are in good company—the rest of the earth's beings are doing their part to mend too. Bees use propolis to repair a crack in the hive, a forest regrows after a fire, spiders fix a damaged web, a fox nurses her wounds. Given the opportunity, nature repairs itself. In time, it restores. Where soil is laid bare, by tilling, by clear-cut, landslide, or some other disruptive act, immediately very hardy plants burst forth to begin a chain of ecological succession that will eventually reinstate a biodiverse system.

Mending is a transformative practice—a small, meditative act that sends ripples of loving-kindness out into the world around the mender. Small acts matter in the slow process of culture change and should never be discounted as unworthy. These small acts make new futures possible, and we can do them every day.

When you walk through the world with a mend on your clothes, you should feel incredibly proud of your ingenuity and resiliency. You are wearing your gratitude, your convictions. You are healing in a small but very big way, and it's beautiful.

—Nina & Sonya

Acknowledgments

+ + + + + + +

First, we'd like to extend enormous gratitude once again to our parents. Your philosophies have greatly informed our approach to mending and making art. Thanks to you, Mama, for teaching us to sew and for keeping our spirits up with your constant cheerleading. As Pa always says, you are like a cork on the sea. And thank you, Pa, for your ever-insightful anecdotes. And for your red thread.

A very special thanks to Joseph Kieffer, for arriving on our doorstep on a rainy day and offering to fix our things. You probably don't realize what a sign of affirmation from the universe you were for us!

We couldn't have made this book without the everlasting support of Nolan Calisch, who on a daily basis generously gave me (Nina) the gift of time to work. Thank you, Nols, for all the nourishing meals and walks with Lu. You are the glue that has held us all together over the past year.

Sweet Lucia, your luminous smiles brought levity to the room count-less times when we were making this book. You are a bright, shining light for us all.

A heartfelt thank-you to Susan Roxborough, our editor, for believing in our ability to inspire and teach people to mend and for giving us creative freedom with this book.

Our gratitude to you, Kate Woodrow, for your confidence in us and steadfastness of support and for helping this book find a home in the world.

Sincere thanks to Julie Derrick and Colleen Tretter for generously offer-ing your special repair knowledge for this book. What you give to the world is the coolest.

Lastly, a *big* thank-you to everyone who supported our little home-made mending zine, the first version of this book. You led us down this beautiful path.

Notes

+ + + + + +

1 "Microfiber Masses Recovered from Conventional Machine Washing of New or Aged Garments," by Niko L. Hartline et al. (*Environmental Science and Technology*, 2016). A UC Santa Barbara study, commissioned by Patagonia, found that a single fleece jacket could release as many as 250,000 plastic fibers in a single machine wash.

2 "New Study Finds Widespread Plastic Microfiber Contamination in Bottled Water," by Stiv Wilson (StoryofStuff.org, 2018). A study commissioned by The Story of Stuff Project found microfiber contamination in nineteen different commercial bottled waters.

3 *Braiding Sweetgrass: Indigenous Wisdom, Scientific Knowledge, and the Teachings of Plants* by Robin Wall Kimmerer (Minneapolis: Milkweed Editions, 2013).

Resources

+ + + + + + +

Books

Overdressed: The Shockingly High Cost of Cheap Fashion by Elizabeth L. Cline. A book exploring the myriad of issues around the fast fashion industry and what we can do to counter the disposable fashion culture.

Simple Crocheting by Erika Knight. Straightforward instructions for how to crochet with accessible projects.

Simple Knitting by Erika Knight. Straightforward instructions for how to knit with accessible projects.

The Ultimate Sashiko Sourcebook by Susan Briscoe. Go deeper into sashiko.

+ + + + + + +

Online Resources

Fashion Revolution. FashionRevolution.org. An international movement calling for a more transparent, sustainable, and fair fashion industry.

Julie Derrick, JD's Shoe Repair. JDShoeRepair.com. You can mail your shoes (or backpacks, bags, belts, and more) to JD for excellent repair.

Patagonia's Worn Wear. WornWear.Patagonia.com. Repair, share, and recycle outdoor gear.

The Repair Association. Repair.org. Join the Right to Repair movement! Many states have proposed Right to Repair bills, which require manufacturers to disclose repair information and provide parts to third-party repair businesses and product owners. That means every time a replaceable part breaks, owners aren't forced to buy new.

The Story of Stuff Project. StoryofStuff.org. An international coalition of changemakers exploring the intricacies of key issues in our time, including overconsumption and microfibers.

The True Cost, directed by Andrew Morgan. TrueCostMovie.com. A documentary exposing how the fast fashion industry has impacted workers, the environment, and consumers.

Inspiration

+ + + + + + +

Books

Cradle to Cradle: Remaking the Way We Make Things by William McDonough and Michael Braungart. An exploration of how we could model our entire systems of production after nature, shifting away from massive wasteful-ness to elegant design and processes that "close the loop" completely.

Emergent Strategy: Shaping Change, Changing Worlds by adrienne maree brown. Drawing from patterns found in nature and the writing of Octavia Butler, this book is a radical toolkit for transformation in challenging times.

A Handmade Life: In Search of Simplicity by William Coperthwaite. A wise elder's essays on work, play, beauty, raising children, how to cultivate a more personal sense of the world, and much more.

In Praise of Shadows by Jun'ichirō Tanizaki. In this compelling exploration of the differences between Eastern and Western aesthetics, Tanizaki invites us into a world of subtlety and mindfulness.

Letters to Vanessa: On Love, Science, and Awareness in an Enchanted World by Jeremy W. Hayward. In tender letters to his daughter, Hayward disrupts the stories upon which much of our Western culture is built: survival of the fittest, human superiority, and the presumption that the inanimate world is insentient.

The Man Who Created Paradise: A Fable by Gene Logsdon. A poignant agrarian tale about stewardship and regenerative agriculture.

The More Beautiful World Our Hearts Know Is Possible by Charles Eisenstein. A powerful antidote to the despair and paralysis we feel, this book reveals how many of the world's problems stem from a deeply entrenched underlying story of separation and invites us to lean into a recognition of interbeing, trusting that small acts reverberate throughout the world.

Radical Homemakers: Reclaiming Domesticity from a Consumer Culture by Shannon Hayes. A collection of inspiring case studies of people who have redefined their sense of livelihood and relationship to work.

Wabi-Sabi for Artists, Designers, Poets & Philosophers by Leonard Koren. A slim volume that illuminates the Japanese aesthetic universe of *wabi-sabi* and guides our hearts and minds toward embracing the imperfect, impermanent, and the humble.

+ + + + + +

Further Inspiration

iFixit's Repair Manifesto. iFixit.com/Manifesto. iFixit is a wiki-based website that provides instructions for how to fix almost anything. Users can create a repair manual for any device; they can also edit existing manuals to improve them.

Machines, directed by Rahul Jain. Machines-theMovie.com. An artful documentary following the lives of workers in a giant garment factory in Gujarat, India.

Mottainai Campaign. GreenBeltMovement.org. The Japanese concept of *mottainai* (nothing should be wasted and all things should be used with gratitude) inspired Wangari Maathai's Mottainai Campaign to eliminate plastic waste in Kenya.

Tom of Holland. TomofHolland.com. The Visible Mending Programme is dedicated to reviving traditional mending techniques.

Index

+ + + + + + +

G

glove darners (tool), 6, 12
gloves, darning techniques for, 66–67

H

Hari-Kuyō (Festival of Broken Needles), 153
hemming pants, 154–159
hems, patching. *See* cuffs, patching
holes, patching techniques for, 95–103

I

Interior Patch
    Exposed Edge Technique, 101–103
    Tucked Edge Technique, 99–100
irons, 6, 8

J

jackets
    adding a pocket, 166–170
    mending down jackets, 104–107
    patching cuffs, 108–110
jogakbo (Korean traditional patch-work), 75

K

kintsugi ("golden joinery"), 13
knit versus woven fabric, 16–17
Knitted Patch, 79–81
knitting needles, 6, 12
knots, tying
    overhand knots at the end of your thread, 22–23
    square knots to continue sewing, 24–25
    stitching in place to finish sewing, 26
    techniques for darning, 55–56
    when to use, 22

L

leggings, mending, 132–133
linens, patching, 111

M

mending
    animism, 153
    basic skills, 20–26
    basic stitches, 27–31
    considering every garment, vi
    fabric, right side versus wrong side, 154
    fabric basics, 16–19
    as form of healing, xxv–xxvi, 180
    on the go, 14–15
    noticing early signs of wear, 19
    open letter to the woman who made my shirt, 172

U

underarm holes, mending, 138–139

— — — —

W

whip stitch, 28–29
wool roving, 7, 12
work wear, 135
woven versus knit fabric, 16–17

— — — —

Y

yarn, 6, 10

— — — —

Z

zipper repair, 146–149

About the Authors

+ + + + + + +

Sonya and Nina Montenegro

are sisters, as well as illustrators, printmakers, sewers, puppeteers, nature nerds, dreamers, and lifelong students of gardening, beekeeping, and land remediation. Being oriented toward the arts and the natural world explains why we love and appreciate mending. It is a blend of the creative, the practical, and the conscientious.

Famed harmonist Emmylou Harris told the *Telegraph* in a 2006 interview that "when you put two voices together, a third voice is created, and it's always unique." Each of us has always been an artist independently, but we have come to recognize the strength of our shared "third" voice, and in 2013 we formalized our artistic collaboration as The Far Woods (TheFarWoods.com). The artwork we create is grounded in our understanding that the time has come for humans to come into right relationship with the earth and with one another. We aim to elevate the principles of compassion, interbeing, mutual flourishing, collaboration, biodiversity, and reciprocity. A screen printer friend once said that every time she pulls a print it feels like she is sending up a prayer. We feel this way when we mend. In every mended garment, there is an understanding of its role in the manifestation of the world we want future generations to inhabit.

Printed in China

SASQUATCH BOOKS with colophon is a registered trademark of Penguin Random House LLC

24 23 22 21   9 8 7 6 5 4 3

Editor: Susan Roxborough
Production editor: Jill Saginario
Designer: Bryce de Flamand
Production designer: Alison Keefe

Library of Congress Cataloging-in-Publication Data
Names: Montenegro, Nina, author. | Montenegro, Sonya, author.
Title: Mending life : a handbook for repairing clothes and hearts / Nina and
   Sonya Montenegro.
Description: Seattle, WA : Sasquatch Books, [2020] | Includes bibliographical
   references and index.
Identifiers: LCCN 2019015016 | ISBN 9781632172525 (hard cover)
Subjects: LCSH: Clothing and dress--Repairing--Handbooks, manuals, etc.
Classification: LCC TT720 .M66 2020 | DDC 646/.3--dc23
LC record available at https://lccn.loc.gov/2019015016

ISBN: 978-1-63217-252-5

Sasquatch Books
1904 Third Avenue, Suite 710
Seattle, WA 98101

SasquatchBooks.com